Living and Leading by Faith

Strategies for Victorious Christian Living
from the Book of Joshua

Dr. Jerry Harmon

Sermon To Book
www.sermontobook.com

Living and Leading by Faith / Dr. Jerry Harmon
ISBN-13: 978-1-952602-38-2

Praise for *Living and Leading by Faith* by Dr. Jerry Harmon

Today there is a dearth of good Bible exposition. Dr. Harmon helps correct that. His excellent exposition of Joshua is a wonderful example of how to expound the meaning of a passage of Scripture and apply it to our contemporary circumstances. Read this [for your] great personal profit.

Jerry Vines
Pastor Emeritus, First Baptist Church, Jacksonville, FL
President and Chairman of the Board of Jerry Vines Ministries, Inc.

In describing the beloved founding pastor of Grace Bible Baptist Church in Baltimore, Maryland, his successor, Dr. Jerry Harmon lovingly stated, "he was General Patton with a KJV." I knew Dr. Johnson. Earl was a dear, precious friend. Jerry's description is spot on.

I must also say, his successor is a splendid man of God. I would, therefore, say of Jerry Harmon, "he is Dwight Eisenhower with a Ph.D." Dwight Eisenhower served two terms as America's president at what author Paul Johnson stated was "the climax of the American century." Eisenhower was exactly what America needed for the decade of the 1950s. Dr. Jerry Harmon is exactly what is needed at Grace Bible Baptist Church as he follows his pastor's legacy. He is a preacher with precision in exposition [and] a heart for the story of Grace Baptist, and like Joshua of old, will lead many into their promised land of victorious Christian living.

As you read [this book], you will experience this in your own life. Dr. Harmon knows this subject well. He has been there and [worked] with a man as respected by those who knew him as Moses was to the children of Israel. To my dear friend, Dr. Jerry Harmon, thank you for this excellent contribution to all who read this life-changing story.

Dino Pedrone, D.Min.
DPM Ministries, Delray Beach, Florida

Dr. Jerry Harmon begins this book by recalling a trip to Camp of the Nations. I was the founder and director of that camp, and I vividly recall the enthusiastic young man with bright red hair who arrived on the bus that day. He was brimming over with the joy of his newfound faith, and his loyalty and love for Pastor Johnson was just as evident. A disciple is one who becomes like his master, and Dr. Harmon mirrors, in many ways, the character of his predecessor. Different in temperament, but with the same devotion to the Scriptures and love for the people he now pastors as his predecessor had.

Dr. Jerry Harmon is known in his own right, both here in the States and internationally, as a careful and capable exegete of the Word of God. His ministry is sought after because his heart is in tune with the Author of the Book. I am delighted that he has taken up the mantle and is teaching us as he himself was taught. I expect this book to be a tremendous blessing to all who read it.

Dr. William K. Shade
Former Director of Source of Light Ministries International, Madison, GA
Founder of World Wide Bible Institute

To Dr. Earl M. Johnson, Jr., Founding Pastor of Grace Bible Baptist Church, spiritual father, mentor, and true warrior for Christ. Thank you for demonstrating victorious Christian living to us all and teaching us how to live and lead by faith.

To the loving and faithful congregation of Grace Bible Baptist Church. Thank you for extending to me the same love and honor that you gave to Pastor Johnson, our Moses.

CONTENTS

Stay Faithful to Christ

The summer of 1978 was a turning point in my life. It was the summer my father was converted to faith in Jesus Christ. I *saw* the power of the gospel before I ever heard it. My dad was a new man, and everyone in the family knew it. My mother was right there beside him and placed her faith in Christ as well. This was the fulfillment of what she had always wanted and the answer to her prayers. The grace of God had entered into the Harmon household, and none of us would be the same.

In time, I came to understand the gospel and my need as a sinner to repent of my sin and to place my trust in the atoning work of Christ. As a fifteen-year-old kid, I did just that. Not long afterward, I went to Christian summer camp for a week. I had never been to summer camp before, let alone Christian camp. God would use that experience to work in my heart in a profound way.

It began on the five-hour van ride. As a new believer, I read the Bible voraciously. I will never forget reading through the Gospel of Matthew with the new Bible my mother bought for me. I saw the beauty and gentleness of

Christ, and it moved me deeply. While riding in the van on the way to Camp of the Nations in South Gibson, PA, I began reading the Old Testament book of Joshua. I already knew Jesus, and I knew of Moses from watching the movie *The Ten Commandments*, but Joshua was another story. I was anxious to learn about him.

I came to learn that the main character in the book of Joshua was not Joshua; it was God. It was all about the mighty work God did through Joshua. This idea was revealed to me as I read the first few verses in the first chapter. Do you ever feel a verse jump off the page and into your heart when you are reading Scripture? That's what it felt like to me when I came to verse 5: "There shall not any man be able to stand before thee all the days of thy life: as I was with Moses, so I will be with thee: I will not fail thee, nor forsake thee" (Joshua 1:5). What an awesome verse!

It was particularly appealing to a fifteen-year-old kid who played running back in football. Obviously, that's not what God meant. I began to see that Joshua was called to take possession of a land that was filled with giants led by kings with formidable armies. All these things represented challenges and hindrances for Joshua in fulfilling his God-given task. God was giving Joshua a sweeping promise of victory over all those challenges.

As I grew older, I began to see that life is filled with "giants." Challenges await in every season, around every turn, and in every facet of this life. They tower over us and forbid us to take possession of our God-given lot. The good news is that the promise God gave Joshua still applies to us today.

The verse that found me when I was 15 has never left my heart. I have to refer back to it when a new giant calls out to me. Eventually, as I grew in my relationship with God, I learned how to apply that promise. In essence, that's what the book of Joshua is all about. It teaches us how to claim this God-given victory. For every New Testament truth, there is an Old Testament illustration. The book of Joshua is the illustration of the truth that "we are more than conquerors through him that loved us" (Romans 8:37).

Recently, however, Joshua 1:5 has taken on a new meaning for me. I have especially come to love and cling to the second part of the verse: "...as I was with Moses, so I will be with thee." In 2012, I was called to come home and be the Senior Pastor of the church where I was saved and grew in Christ. My home church, Grace Bible Baptist Church, was started and pastored by Dr. Earl M. Johnson, Jr., one of God's great servants.

Pastor Johnson was a Korean War vet from New Jersey. He was saved while he was in the military, and after the war, God used him to start several churches and run the serviceman's center in Aberdeen, MD. There's no way to put a number to the young men God used him to impact for Christ. Many are in the ministry today because of his ministry. My family and I were saved under his powerful preaching. I also surrendered to the call to preach under his leadership and learned about ministry just from being around him.

My first job at Grace was as a janitor. Pastor Johnson hired me for fifty dollars a week. I thought I was rich, and in truth, I was. I was at the church every day, doing any and every menial task he required. I counted it a privilege to empty his trash, clean his office, run errands for him, and anything else he asked. I observed firsthand his passion for ministry, his devotion, the long hours he invested, the battles he fought, the difficult decisions he had to make, and the victories he won.

Under his ministry, Grace Bible Baptist Church grew from a handful of people in a small building to a large, influential congregation several buildings later. His ministry included many years of radio broadcasting and thirteen years of the TV ministry "The Everliving Story." I have never met anyone who better exemplified the principles of victorious Christian living than Pastor Johnson. He lived it! I merely write about it and, by God's grace, also try to apply it. To the good people of Grace and to me, Pastor Johnson was our Moses.

When his health began to decline, he asked me to come and eventually take the mantle of leadership for Grace. Following a great man is not easy. You can imagine my reluctance. At the time, I pastored a church in Tennessee and had no desire to move back to Maryland. Honestly, I went back and forth over the decision, but God providentially made it clear what He wanted.

I moved to Maryland and shared ministry duties with Pastor Johnson, and I gradually transitioned into the role of Senior Pastor. Pastor Johnson stepped down and became Founding Pastor. Even during his declining years, he still actively loved and served the sheep at Grace. I gave him a platform to preach as much as I could and as his own health would allow. I know that typically when a new, young lion takes charge of the pride, he doesn't want the old lion around anymore. There's some kind of unwritten rule about that among pastors. New pastor comes; old pastor must go away and never be seen or heard. To me, this didn't make sense, at least in our situation. It wasn't my desire, nor the desire of the congregation at Grace. I wanted him around. His mere presence was an encouragement and inspiration. Yes, he did do some Monday morning quarterbacking, but nothing over the top. Besides, that's to be expected from a man I thought was the strongest and most courageous Christian leader I ever met. When people asked me what kind of leader he was, I would respond, "He was General Patton with a KJV." Pastor Johnson sat on the front row, encouraging the congregation and me to keep the tanks moving forward and to stay faithful to Christ. We all could see his decline in health and knew this splendid soldier wouldn't be here much longer. One Sunday morning after closing prayer, Pastor Johnson asked for a mic. He then announced that it was his last Sunday at Grace.

He told the congregation that if anyone wanted to say a last "goodbye" to him, he would be in the front. The line to his wheelchair went around the sanctuary as people whose lives he touched waited to give their final salute. Indeed, that was his last Sunday. A few days later, our Moses, my Moses, scaled Mount Pisgah's lofty height, viewed his home, and took his flight. His robe of flesh was dropped so he could rise and seize his everlasting prize. The privilege of my life was to preach his homegoing service to a packed, standing-room-only auditorium of people who dearly loved him.

I must confess that I thought I was ready for that, and in a way, I was, but it hurt. Our church grieved together. In my heart, I felt not only empty, but a bit lost. Pastor Johnson had started the church and pastored it faithfully for over forty-three years, then served as Founding Pastor till his dying day. It was hard to imagine Grace Bible Baptist Church without Dr. Earl M. Johnson, Jr. As the great theologian Rocky Balboa said, "If you stay in one place long enough, you become that place."[1]

To some, Pastor Johnson was Grace, and Grace was Pastor Johnson. But he was gone. I felt not only the same sorrow as the congregation, but also the weight of the world on my shoulders. Just then, God whispered the words of Joshua 1:5 into my heart: "As I was with Moses, so I will be with thee: I will not fail thee, nor forsake thee." God placed that verse in my heart when I was 15 because He knew I would need it for such a time as this. It has become the rock I stand upon during the difficult days and the comforting pillow I lay my head upon in the dark nights.

During all these events I described, I preached through the book of Joshua to the loving congregation of Grace. It seemed appropriate. I knew I needed it, even if no one else did. Although Pastor Johnson is gone, there still remains much land to possess, more victories to be won, more giants that must fall, more impossible rivers to cross, and more strongholds to conquer. He showed us how to do it. His triumphant life in Christ is reflected in the victorious overtones of the book of Joshua.

May you and I experience victory as we learn to live and lead by faith like he did. But he would be the first to say, "It wasn't me. It was all Christ!" That's what we all must remember. It wasn't Moses; it was God. If anything lasting takes place in the future, it won't be due to Joshua. It will be because Joshua learned to trust in God the same way Moses did.

The chapters of this book are drawn from sermons in the series I preached through the book of Joshua at Grace. Each chapter begins with a "Big Idea" to summarize the major overall point. This is the homiletics professor part of me coming out. I have always taught students in my

Expository Preaching classes to make sure to communicate clearly the one major idea of the sermon. I would remind them, "If you can't give the sermon in one sentence, you are not ready to preach it."

Each Big Idea is like a sermon in a sentence, and it's given to aid readers and preachers alike. Each chapter concludes with application-focused questions as well as a suggested journal prompt and an action step so that you can personalize the life-changing truths found in the stories of Joshua, Rahab, Caleb, and others. My prayer is that God will use this book to help you see that in Christ you are already victorious against the giants you must face. No stronghold can hinder you from fully possessing your spiritual heritage and blessing in Christ if you will just claim it by faith. May you chase away all your giants, may all your strongholds fall, and may all your rivers be divided as you apply these principles and live and lead by faith.

CHAPTER ONE

Victorious Christian Living
Joshua 1:1–9

Big Idea: For Christians, victory is not our destination, but rather our point of origin.

Now thanks be unto God, which always causeth us to triumph in Christ, and maketh manifest the savour of his knowledge by us in every place.

—2 Corinthians 2:14

June 1944—it was the day of the great battle. Thousands of men in thousands of ships and planes were awaiting their orders when they heard the broadcasted voice of the Supreme Commander of the Allied Forces in Europe. He told them:[2]

I have full confidence in your courage, devotion to duty and skill in battle. We will accept nothing less than full Victory!

Good luck! And let us beseech the blessing of Almighty
God upon this great and noble undertaking.
  —General Dwight Eisenhower, June 6, 1944

Hours later, wave after wave of men got out of the
boats into the water and slogged onto the beaches of
France. They dropped out of planes in hostile and unforgiving terrain behind enemy lines. They all fought the
battle that would turn the tide of the war, persevering
against staggering odds because they believed they could
win. It was D-Day.

1400 B.C.[3]—the book of Joshua tells us of another battle of impossible odds as the Israelites prepared to enter
the promised land. They had to cross a river at flood stage
and face a nation of giants in a fortified city with great
stone walls. They were on the outside looking in, and few
had experience in battle, but they had to win Jericho if
they were going to move into the land God had given
them. It looked grim. Joshua had to wait for a word from
his Supreme Commander, God.

God promised Joshua a complete and total victory and
gave him the winning strategy. Joshua only had to believe
and trust God. What God said to Joshua so very long ago
still applies to you. You may be thinking, *"What does a
military invasion that took place thousands of years ago
have to do with my life today? What do an uncrossable
river and armies of formidable giants have to do with
me?"* The Apostle Paul would say, "It has everything to
do with you." In Romans 15:4, he wrote, "For whatsoever
things were written aforetime were written for our learning, that we through patience and comfort of the scriptures

might have hope." Learning about how Joshua faced these huge challenges gives hope to people like you and me.

You, too, probably have rivers in your life that you can't cross, giants blocking your path, and mountains that you can't figure out how to get around or tunnel through. We all do. But just as God promised victory for Joshua, He has promised victory for all His children. The key is simply to realize that the victory has already been provided. God wants you to know this, and He wants you to have a confident attitude that says, "I will accept nothing less than complete, total victory for my life." The great theme of the book of Joshua that one must learn is this: you have the victory, and God expects you to live in that victory.

You may be thinking, *"Well, I know some Christians who aren't living in victory."* I do, too, but that's not God's plan. God's plan is for you and me to live according to the privileges that He has given us. While the Bible admits the *possibility* of failure, it never assumes the *necessity* of failure. If you are not living victoriously, you are living beneath all that God has for you.

The theme of the book of Joshua is victory in the life of God's people. As we study this and other books of the Old Testament, they teach us the principles of God through human example, and they encourage us.

Who Was Joshua?

We are introduced to Joshua in the story of the Israelites' exodus from Egypt under the leadership of Moses. In Exodus 24:13, Joshua is called Moses' "assistant" (ESV,

NKJV) or servant. Born a slave in Egypt, Joshua followed Moses throughout the nation of Israel's difficult wilderness experience. Moses must have seen something very special about him, because he made Joshua his closest aide. Joshua accompanied Moses on Mount Sinai. No doubt Joshua learned much from Moses simply by serving at his side. When Moses set up a special tent where he and God could commune, Joshua stayed just outside, guarding the tent (Exodus 33:7–11).

Joshua was a soldier. He led the army of Israel in battle against Amalek, as recorded in Exodus 17:8–16. Joshua's role in the conflict with Amalek was preparation for the many battles he would fight in the promised land.[4]

Joshua was also a spy. When Moses sent twelve men to spy out the land of Canaan, Joshua was one of those spies. He and Caleb gave a good report, but the others gave an evil report (Numbers 13–14). The people should have listened to Joshua and Caleb, not to the faithless ten spies. It was this act of unbelief and rebellion that delayed entry into the promised land for forty years.[5]

After many years of serving at the side of Moses and observing his life, Joshua became a leader and a man of God. Perhaps Joshua didn't know it, but God had been preparing him to take the mantle of leadership from Moses. A.W. Tozer said, "God rarely projects his chosen servants to suddenly burst upon the world without previous preparation. Most will be found to have spent a long apprenticeship to God somewhere before being entrusted with the important work."[6] God spent eighty years preparing Joshua in Egypt, in the wilderness, and in Canaan. Joshua became a great spiritual leader who led Israel to victory, not because of his skill with the sword but because of his submission to the Word of God (Joshua 1:8) and the God of the Word (Joshua 5:13–15).

Comparing Joshua to Jesus

For if Joshua had given them rest, God would not have spoken of another day later on.

—Hebrews 4:8 *(ESV)*

In the New Testament, the author of Hebrews referred to the "rest" that the children of Israel entered into because of the victories won by Joshua. The inspired writer explained that when Joshua led the people into the promised land, it was a picture of the *rest* of salvation provided by Jesus Christ. The *rest* of the promised land pointed to the ultimate *rest* a person may enter into by faith in the work of Christ.

The writer of Hebrews skillfully wove together two Old Testament passages to make his point. He referred to Joshua's conquest in the book of Joshua, and he quoted Psalm 95:11 in Hebrews 4:3 (ESV):

*For we who have believed enter that rest, as he has said,
"As I swore in my wrath, 'They shall not enter my rest,'"
although his works were finished from the foundation of
the world.*

Even those who entered the promised land under Joshua didn't experience the fullness of God's rest. How do we know that? Later on, three hundred years after Joshua, David spoke of the need to enter into God's rest. If Joshua had given the children of Israel ultimate rest, then why did David speak of a rest that was still needed? The answer is that the rest provided by Joshua was but a picture of the ultimate rest of salvation provided by Jesus Christ.

In this manner, Joshua is a picture of Jesus Christ. *Jesus* is the Greek version of the Old Testament Hebrew name *Joshua*.[7] Both names, Jesus and Joshua, mean "Jehovah saves."[8] The original readers of the epistle of Hebrews would have seen the play on names and made the mental connection. Just as the people of Israel rested in the victory already provided for them under Joshua, the believer today rests in the work of Christ for salvation and victory. Joshua defeated Israel's earthly foes. Jesus defeats our heavenly foes. Joshua brought Israel to the land of Canaan, and Jesus brings us to our victory and rest. Joshua's counsel was rejected at Kadesh Barnea. Jesus came to His own people, and they did not receive Him. Joshua brought military victory for Israel. Jesus brings victory over sin and death for all who believe in Him.

The principle the writer of Hebrews was emphasizing is faith. The people in Joshua's day had to exercise faith in the victory God had already provided. Today we must exercise faith in the victory provided for us by Jesus Christ. How does one do that? How do we exercise faith in the victory already won?

Five Principles for Living in Victory

In the very first chapter of the book of Joshua, we can distinguish five principles God gave to Joshua that still apply to us today as we seek to claim by faith the victory won for us.

1. Don't Live in the Past

> *Now after the death of Moses the servant of the LORD it came to pass, that the LORD spake unto Joshua the son of Nun, Moses' minister, saying, Moses my servant is dead; now therefore arise, go over this Jordan, thou, and all this people, unto the land which I do give to them, even to the children of Israel.*
>
> *—Joshua 1:1–2*

God's servants pass on. God's work continues. God doesn't want you to be looking in the past all the time. While it may be good at times to use the past as a reference, you can't dwell in the past. The past must function like a rudder to guide us into the future, rather than an anchor to weigh us down. I don't write these words superficially. I am purposeful in putting this into practice in my own life. I have the tendency to look backward in life, rather than forward. It's part of my sentimental personality and a result of the circumstances I have lived.

I serve as the Senior Pastor of Grace Bible Baptist Church in Baltimore, Maryland. This is the very church where I first heard the gospel and was saved. I saw the power of the gospel transform the lives of my father and mother under the preaching of Dr. Earl M. Johnson, Jr., the founding pastor of Grace. He was a powerful preacher of the Word and a strong leader. In 1972, Pastor Johnson and a handful of other people bought the campus where the church presently meets. I still remember the story Pastor Johnson told of how he walked around the prospective campus, praying, and with each footstep claimed the land for God's glory.

At that time, he and the small congregation of Grace had no money, but they believed God wanted a church there. Long story short, God providentially honored Pastor Johnson's faith. Forty-eight years and many building programs later, the campus of many buildings and a large sanctuary is paid in full. In his years of faithful service, many have been converted, and many have been called to ministry. I represent one of them.

As I mentioned in the introduction, Pastor Johnson hired me to be the church janitor when I was fifteen years old. This afforded me the privilege of being at church all the time and observing him in action. He was truly a man of faith and a bold leader. Much of what I know about ministry and leadership I learned from his godly example. After college, seminary, and years of my own pastoral ministry, Pastor Johnson invited me to come back to Grace and take the mantle of leadership.

When I finally agreed to pick up his mantle and become Senior Pastor, I knew I wanted him to stay around. I couldn't imagine our church without his presence. I know some incoming pastors are not comfortable with the old pastor staying around, critiquing and playing "Monday-morning quarterback." But I didn't feel that way at all with Pastor Johnson, and neither did the Grace family. He was the only pastor Grace had ever known up until me.

In a way, he was like our Moses. He kept the title of Founding Pastor and an office at the church until the day the Lord called him home. When God did finally call His faithful soldier home, it was hard for our church. It was hard on me! We all needed time just to grieve. Even today, I still wander over to his empty office and find myself going in, wishing I could talk with him again and reminiscing about the past and the way things were. It's been hard to accept Grace without Pastor Johnson, but I am sure it was even harder for Joshua and the people to imagine an Israel without Moses. We all have certain past events and experiences that make it difficult for us to move forward and not live in the past.

This is why God's word to Joshua was so important when He said, "Moses my servant is dead; now therefore arise, go over this Jordan" (Joshua 1:2). The death of a faithful servant needs to serve as a motivation to go forward in faith. I still remember the words I heard Pastor Johnson say many times: "God's servants pass on. God's work continues." In the case of Joshua, it was: "God's servant passed on. God's people must pass over." We best honor past servants by our present and future faithfulness, so make a decision that you will not let the past chain you. Determine to exercise the same faith that you observed in the lives of godly servants.

The Apostle Paul wrote:

Brethren, I count not myself to have apprehended: but this one thing I do, forgetting those things which are behind,

and reaching forth unto those things which are before....
—Philippians 3:13

Paul wasn't saying that you should never look back; he was saying that you should never let the past distract you. You don't need to delve into the hurts of the past. It can be helpful to reflect on what happened to you in the past in order to understand where you are in the present and where you need to grow, but if all you do is look to the past, you will have no future. There's nothing in the Bible that tells you to go back and nurse all those old wounds. No, the Bible tells you to look forward and to go forward.

Some people are haunted by past guilt. All great Christians whom God has used have experienced past failures, but they didn't allow the regret of those failures to keep them down! All of us have regrets. If you continue to think and live on that, it will zap all of your energy for the future.

Some people live with past glory. If God has done great things for you in the past, you should rejoice, but you can't live on past victory. If you look too much into the past, you are going to freeze. For some people, it's past grief. Thank God for His comfort that helps you through those things, but some people don't want to let those sorrows go. They want to continue to live in those sorrows. If you live in sorrow, you will never have victory in the future.

There are also past grudges. You might have been hurt and be holding a grudge. You will not have victory in the future as long as you are nursing that grudge. Churchill said, "If we open a quarrel between the past and the pre sent we shall find that we have lost the future."[9] That is true in the Christian life as well.

2. Remember That God Has Already Given You the Victory

Every place that the sole of your foot shall tread upon, that have I given unto you, as I said unto Moses.
—Joshua 1:3

It's important to see that God had already given them the land. Even before they crossed over the Jordan, God said to Joshua, "I want you to know this land has already been given to you. It's already yours."

On August 25, 1737, the Colonial authorities of Pennsylvania claimed to have found a lost treaty from 1686 between William Penn, the founder of the colony of Pennsylvania, and the Delaware Indians, the tribe most friendly to William Penn. The treaty said that the Delaware Indians would give to William Penn as much of the tribal land, between the fork of the Delaware and Lehigh rivers, as a man could walk in one and a half days. William Penn's son Thomas hired the three fastest walkers in the colony and offered a considerable prize to the one who covered the most territory. The winner covered more than twice the land the Delaware Indians anticipated, causing the tribe to lose 1,200 square miles of their land. This event has become known as the Walking Purchase.[10]

God wasn't saying to Joshua, "I am going to give you the land that the soles of your feet will tread upon." God was saying to Joshua, "The land that you walk on is already yours." The promised land was not a "Walking Purchase," but rather a "Walking Promise." God had already promised it to them. There was no need for Joshua to hire the fastest walkers in Israel. God was saying, "Just go, and wherever you happen to walk in the land, know that it has already been promised. You simply claim it by faith." Similarly, the Christian life is walking on ground already conquered by Christ. It is recognizing this fact and acting on it in faith.

Canaan is not heaven. Some hymns liken physical death to crossing the Jordan and the land of Canaan to heaven. For the Christian, Canaan represents our spiritual heritage in Christ (Ephesians 1:3, 11, 15–23) as opposed to entering heaven. There are important differences between what the Israelites experienced when they reached Canaan and what we will experience when we get to heaven.

For instance, when Joshua and Israel crossed over the river Jordan, they had to face giants. They had battles to fight. They had defeats and committed sin, even in that promised land. You won't have any of that in heaven. You won't have any battles or giants to face. There will be no defeats or sin in heaven. That will all be gone.

Alan Redpath claimed that the book of Joshua is to the Old Testament what the book of Ephesians is to the New Testament.[11] Ephesians talks about our wealth, our walk, and our warfare. It talks about all the wealth and treasure we have in Christ, about how we are to walk in the Christian life, and about how we have warfare against an enemy.

What Paul's letter to the Ephesians explains doctrinally the book of Joshua illustrates practically. The land of Canaan represents your spiritual inheritance on earth, a victory you must claim. As a believer, victory is not your destination. It is your beginning point. You don't fight *for* victory; you fight *from* victory. Victory is already yours. It's like a coupon or a savings bond—all you need to do is cash it in!

Canaan is release, refreshment, and reality. Canaan represents release. Up until this time, the Israelites had been a nation of slaves. They were about to be free. There would be no more manna. They were about to get something new in their lives. There are times in your life as a believer when you just need something new from God. The old isn't bad; you just need refreshing from the Lord.

Canaan represents rest. In Hebrews 4, the Bible refers to Canaan as a place of rest. Now, this is not rest from activity. It's not rest from work. It's rest *while* you work. Some Christians are always burnt out! God wants you to learn to rest in Him. As Dr. Warren W. Wiersbe wrote in his book *Be Strong*, "This 'Canaan rest' is a picture of the rest that Christian believers experience when they yield their all to Christ and claim their inheritance by faith."[12]

Canaan represents reality. A lot of times in the Christian life, you will hear sermons about victory and the great things God has done. I don't just want to hear sermons; I want to experience those things. That's what Canaan represents. As the Israelites got ready to cross over, God said, "You have to put the foot of faith in the land of promise and claim it." Then they had their own set of miracles before their eyes.

Satan is already defeated. Christ has already won. Nevertheless, you must place your foot of faith in the land of promise and say, "This is mine, and I claim it in the name of Jesus." The Christian life is simply walking on ground already conquered and owning it!

3. Claim God's Promises

> *There shall not any man be able to stand before thee all the days of thy life: as I was with Moses, so I will be with thee: I will not fail thee, nor forsake thee.*
> —*Joshua 1:5*

God offers His conquering power. Now, this promise from God was very significant to Joshua. When Moses sent the twelve spies to check out the land of Canaan, they came back with the report that the land flowed with milk and honey, but there were giants in the land (Numbers 13:26–33). Joshua was there and saw them. These guys were huge! But God told Joshua, "Don't worry. They are not going to be able to stand before you." That didn't mean it was going to be easy.

When you got saved, you might have thought that everything was going to be easy because you were a Christian. There are times when it's not easy, when there are challenges that seem like giants.

What giants are trying to hold you back? Fear, ego, pride, lust, jealousy, worry, complacency, greed, enslavement? Some say, "I don't have the power to drive them out!" Living victoriously is not your responsibility, but it is your response to His ability. What God demands of you He does through you! These giants cannot stand before you when you live in the power of victory that God is giving you.

God offers His continual presence. God promises concrete power, but He also promises His continual presence. The very first time I read Joshua 1:5, I was in a van going to summer camp. Have you ever read a verse in the Bible that seems to jump off the page? Well, at that time of my life, the Lord used this verse to encourage me to follow Him. As a teenager, I prayed, "Lord, I want You to be with me the way You were with Moses and with Joshua. I want Your presence in my life." Little did I know at that time that I would follow in the footsteps of a great leader, my pastor, and become pastor of my home church or that I would become president of a seminary that was founded in 1937 and had only three presidents prior to me, all great men in their own right.

I know from experience that following in the footsteps of great leaders can cause anxiety and fear. My experience was nothing compared to how Joshua must have felt when he assumed the mantle of Israel's great deliverer, lawgiver, and intercessor. I can only imagine how comforting those words must have been for him: "As I was with Moses, so I will be with thee" (Joshua 1:5).

The central character of the book of Joshua is not Joshua—it's God! If anything worthwhile is accomplished, we know it's not us, but rather the hand of God.

God could accomplish His purpose through Joshua just as well as He could through Moses. The same can be said of you and me. As long as we know that God is with us, we have no reason to be anxious. The Apostle Paul wrote, "Faithful is he that calleth you, who also will do it" (1 Thessalonians 5:24).

The writer of Hebrews quotes this promise in Hebrews 13:5: "...for he hath said, I will never leave thee, nor forsake thee." I like the way the Amplified Bible translates this verse: "...for He has said, 'I WILL NEVER [under any circumstances] DESERT YOU [nor give you up nor leave you without support, nor will I in any degree leave you helpless], NOR WILL I FORSAKE or LET YOU DOWN or RELAX MY HOLD ON YOU [assuredly not]!'" (Hebrews 13:5 AMP).

4. Refuse to Live in Fear

> *Be strong and of a good courage: for unto this people shalt thou divide for an inheritance the land, which I sware unto their fathers to give them. Only be thou strong and very courageous, that thou mayest observe to do according to all the law, which Moses my servant commanded thee: turn not from it to the right hand or to the left, that thou mayest prosper withersoever thou goest. ... Have not I commanded thee? Be strong and of a good courage....*
> —*Joshua 1:6-7, 9*

Today, when we want to emphasize something in writing, we can use bolded or italicized text. We simply highlight the word and click on "bold" or "italics," and the emphasis is made. In Old Testament narrative, repetition served as the literary emphasis. When the writer wanted to hammer an idea into the reader, the expression was repeated. That's what is happening in this narrative, but we also need to remember that the words being repeated are not the words of a narrator or a human character in the story. What's repeated is direct divine speech! If you are familiar with the Old Testament, you know this doesn't happen very often. In the Bible, God didn't often repeat Himself in direct speech to an individual. That's what makes this command so very solemn.

How many times did God say, "Be strong and of a good courage"? Three times! When God says something once, you need to listen. If He says something twice, you really need to pay attention. If He says it three times, you'd better never forget it!

God knew Joshua's heart. God said to Joshua three times, "Be strong." This tells me two things. God knows the hearts of His servants, and God knew Joshua was afraid. We can relate to Joshua, can't we? Moses was dead. Here's a nation of two million Jews that Joshua now had to lead out of the wilderness, across the Jordan River, and into the promised land. He had to help them conquer the Canaanites and push them out of the land. If you have a huge responsibility suddenly thrust upon you, fear is normally your first reaction.

Harry Truman faced a crisis similar to Joshua's. He was a virtually unknown senator from Missouri selected to be Franklin Roosevelt's running mate. On April 12, 1945, after being vice president for only a few months, Truman received a message: "Come to the White House and come as quickly and as quietly as you can." When he got to the White House, he was met by Mrs. Roosevelt in the sitting room, and she said, "Harry, the president died." Truman was too stunned to speak. FDR led the country through a depression and World War II. What would Truman do about Hitler? About Japan? About Stalin and all these major problems? Finally, he managed to ask Mrs. Roosevelt, "Is there anything I can do for you?" She said, "No, Harry, is there anything I can do for you? You're the one who's in trouble now."[13]

I think that's the way Joshua felt. This huge, terrifying responsibility had fallen on him. But God said to Joshua, "Be courageous."

We can choose to be courageous. We don't have to give into our fears. Courage is not the absence of fear; it is the conquest of fear. In fact, it's not really courage unless fear is present. Trust in the Lord as the source of godly courage:

What time I am afraid, I will trust in thee.
—Psalm 56:3

In God have I put my trust: I will not be afraid what man can do unto me.
—Psalm 56:11

Joshua had a choice: he could give into this fear, or he could choose to have faith in God and not be ruled by his fear. At some point in your life, you will need to make a similar choice. If you give into your fears when something overwhelms you, you will be a defeated person, and you will not experience the victory God wants you to have.

Dr. Martyn Lloyd-Jones wrote, "[W]hen a man is defeated by life, it is always due, ultimately, to the fact that he is suffering from [a] spirit of fear. ... [T]his spirit of fear is the real, the ultimate cause of all failure in life, and of all unhappiness."[14]

5. Meditate on God's Word Continually

This book of the law shall not depart out of thy mouth; but thou shalt meditate therein day and night, that thou mayest observe to do according to all that is written therein: for then thou shalt make thy way prosperous, and then thou shalt have good success.

—Joshua 1:8

The Israelites' greatest battle was in the mind. Their biggest enemies were not the Canaanites, but rather sin and self! When they stopped obeying God, they were in trouble. When they gave way to the culture and the sin around them, the battle began. You see, their source of victory was God. They had victory only as long as they obeyed and trusted Him.

The greatest battleground for you as a believer is in your mind. It's imperative for you to stay in God's Word. God says, "Listen, meditate on My Word."

Talk about the Word. God's Word "shall not depart out of thy mouth" (Joshua 1:8). That doesn't mean not to talk about it; it means don't stop talking about it. Keep on talking about the Bible. A problem with some Christians is that they don't talk about the Word of God.

John Bunyan, the great preacher who wrote *The Pilgrim's Progress*, was saved by overhearing the conversation of two women who were talking about the Word of God. If people were to eavesdrop on your conversations, what would they hear?

Think about the Word. "Meditate therein day and night" (Joshua 1:8). When you think of meditation, you may get it confused with Eastern mysticism and yoga. That's not meditation. They teach you to empty your mind. Here, God is telling you to fill your mind with His Word. Meditation can simply mean to speak to yourself or reflect on something. Meditation is like mentally digesting truth. Just coming to church and hearing a sermon is not going to nourish you. You must meditate on it! Meditation can also be singing, like a song that plays over and over in your mind.

Act on the Word. David said in Psalm 39:3, "My heart was hot within me, while I was musing the fire burned: then spake I with my tongue...." Meditation stirs our hearts! The context of this verse is a reference to anger. Something happened that caused David to be angry, and rather than defusing the anger and forgetting the cause, he meditated on it. The result stirred him to action. The principle to learn from this is that meditation inspires action. We will eventually do the things we think about. When God wants to transform us, He never bypasses the brain to go to the heart. We need to have our hearts stirred, but God always goes through the mind—truth in the mind!

Notice where Joshua 1:8 says, "...that thou mayest observe to do according to all that is written therein...." God wants you to meditate because meditation is the key to application. He wants you to think about His Word so that you do it. When you come to church and hear the pastor preach, you download a lot of truth and information. If you just hear and then walk away, and that's it, it's not helping you much. You have to apply it. The bridge between information and application is meditation.

J. I. Packer wrote in his classic, *Knowing God*: "How can we turn our knowledge about God into knowledge of God? The rule for doing this is demanding, but simple. It is that we turn each truth that we learn about God into matter for meditation before God, leading to prayer and praise to God."[15] He added, "Meditation is a lost art today, and Christian people suffer grievously from their ignorance of the practice. Meditation is the activity of calling to mind, and thinking over, and dwelling on, and applying to oneself, the various things that one knows about the works and ways and purposes and promises of God."[16]

If you obey these principles, you will have victory. Don't live in the past. Remember that God is giving you the victory. Claim God's promises. Refuse to live in fear. Meditate on God's Word. Do these things, and whatever giant you have will fall in front of you.

Chapter One Questions

Question: What are some seemingly impossible obstacles or giants that you are facing? What are some areas where you need to experience victory in your life? Where do you need release, refreshment, or to walk in the reality of who you are in Christ? How would believing that God has already given you the victory change your perspective?

_____

_____

_____

_____

_____

_____

_____

_____

_____

Question: In what ways are you tempted to live in the past—guilt, glory, grief, or grudges? How can you remember, learn from, and (where necessary) heal from the past while still moving forward into the future?

_____

_____

_____

_____

_____

_____

_____

_____

_____

Journal: What are some fears that you have about the future, about God's will, concerning your family, or regarding giants that you face? Write out and memorize God's command to be courageous in Joshua 1:9. How does this verse apply to your fears?

_____

_____

_____

_____

_____

_____

_____

_____

_____

Action: What are some specific ways you can talk about, think about, and act on God's Word? How can it be an increasingly significant part of your daily life? Make a list of five to ten ways you can mediate on the truth. Begin to work these ideas into your routine and create new habits around the Bible.

Chapter One Notes

_____

_____

_____

_____

_____

_____

_____

_____

_____

_____

_____

_____

_____

_____

_____

_____

_____

_____

_____

_____

_____

_____

_____

_____

_____

CHAPTER TWO

Learning to Lead
Joshua 1:10–18

Big Idea: *Godly people will not be hindered from following a new leader if they are convinced that he is courageously following God's Word.*

Then Joshua commanded the officers of the people, saying, Pass through the host, and command the people, saying, Prepare you victuals; for within three days ye shall pass over this Jordan, to go in to possess the land, which the LORD your God giveth you to possess it.

—Joshua 1:10–11

S. I. McMillen wrote in his book *None of These Diseases*:[17]

Some time ago I read about a young woman who wanted to go to college. Her heart sank when she read one question on the application blank: "Are you a leader?" Being a conscientious girl she wrote "No" and sent in the form, but she was sure she did not have a chance. To her surprise she received a letter from one of the college officials, which read something like this: "A study of the application forms reveals that this year our college will have 1,452 freshmen leaders. Therefore, we are accepting you because we feel that they have need of at least one follower."

There are many who think of themselves as leaders, but are they truly leaders? Are you a leader? Some say that leaders are born, that it's a natural characteristic. Some argue that leaders are made. It may not come naturally, but they learn to be leaders. Which one is true? I believe both are true. It is true that God gives some people great natural abilities to lead, but it is also true that God makes some people leaders through the school of hard knocks and training. Either way, the common denominator is this: leaders are made by God. In the process of becoming a leader, there's always a bit of a learning curve. Normally it's in a time of crisis that a leader learns valuable lessons and is affirmed.

Joshua came on the scene in a time of great crisis and opposition. It was a time that called for decisive action. After the Lord reassured Joshua that He would be with him just as He had been with Moses (Joshua 1:5), Joshua quickly took charge of his leaders and the people. Joshua was able to provide the spiritual leadership needed at that crucial time in the nation's history.

We are facing a leadership crisis today. Those who are in government seem to have lost the confidence of many of the people they serve. Terrorism is on the rise. Our nation is drifting toward economic disaster and has turned away from God. Where are the preachers who stand up and preach the truth without compromise and are willing to call sin what it is and defend our moral values?

Children are not being trained by their parents. We have passive fathers. We have misguided mothers focused on their careers and neglecting the home. Our school systems are broken. They are more concerned about social issues than teaching students how to read and write, think critically, and develop the basic skills needed for the challenges of the twenty-first century.

Max De Pree, in his book *Leadership Is an Art*, wrote, "Leaders are responsible for future leaders. They need to identify, develop, and nurture future leaders."[18] Our world today is crying out for modern-day Joshuas, men and women who know how to lead.

In my opinion, this is one of the greatest passages in the Old Testament on spiritual leadership. I am surprised that many commentaries simply pass over this section or give it very little attention. From this narrative, we can learn some very important principles from Joshua as we develop our own leadership skills. First, we will focus on some practical principles of leadership, and then we will study the response of the people.

Principles That Forge a Godly Leader

Principle #1—A Leader Must Be in Tune with God

A small but important word is found at the beginning of Joshua 1:10: "Then Joshua commanded...." *Then* is a transitional word that forces us to look back at what happened previously in chapter 1. Joshua had communion with Almighty God and received his orders.

I have the privilege of teaching a seminary class on preaching from Old Testament narratives. One crucial aspect of understanding the plot of any Old Testament narrative is to focus on the speeches made by the characters of the story. Chapter 1 of Joshua consists entirely of four speeches: God speaking to Joshua (verses 1–9), Joshua speaking to the officers (verses 10–11), Joshua speaking to the Transjordan people (verses 12–15), and the people speaking to Joshua (verses 16–18). Each of the speeches in this chapter is a message of encouragement from the speaker, so we can divide chapter 1 simply into three sections: (1) God encouraged Joshua, (2) Joshua encouraged the people, and (3) the people encouraged Joshua.

Joshua was giving the people the plan to cross the Jordan, but notice how it all begins. It begins with Joshua having communion with God, walking with God, and getting his orders from God. As a result, the people were ready to pass into the promised land. When people know a leader is following God, they want to follow. They needed to know Joshua was walking with the Lord the way Moses had walked with the Lord.

After spending time with God, Joshua turned to his officers and got things moving. God's great encouragement gave Joshua courage to face the challenges. To encourage means "to inspire with courage, spirit, or hope: hearten,"[19] and I think Joshua got his heart into his work! Many leaders don't have their hearts in their work because they are not spending time with God.

Principle #2—A Leader Must Be Able to Delegate to Responsible People

Joshua didn't just go right out and talk to the whole of Israel. There was a structure in place. Joshua 1:10 speaks of the "officers" who not only served a military function, but also had responsibilities in civilian government. References are made to this role of "officer" or "taskmaster" in Deuteronomy 16:18 and Exodus 5:6–10. Joshua delegated responsibility and gave authority to trustworthy people under him. Wise leaders know the importance of administration and delegation.

When the great King David died, Solomon had large shoes to fill. Solomon, like Joshua, faced many challenges in his new role. The nation was experiencing population growth during a time of peace for Israel. The government under David needed to be restructured to meet the demands. One night, Solomon made a great sacrifice to God at Gibeon and slept at the altar, perhaps hoping to hear a word from God. God appeared to Solomon in a dream and said, "Ask what I shall give thee" (1 Kings 3:5).

Have you ever heard the expression *carte blanche*? It is French and means, in essence, "blank check." That was God's astonishing offer to Solomon, a blank check for him to fill in. What would you ask God for? Solomon was smart enough to know that he wasn't the leader his father, David, was. He responded by saying, "…I am but a little child: I know not how to go out or come in" (1 Kings 3:7). Knowing how to go out and come in was a Hebrew euphemism for skill in leadership.[2021] David knew how to come out and go in, but Solomon did not.

In this defining moment, Solomon made an incredibly honorable request. Solomon asked for wisdom to lead God's people (1 Kings 3:9–10). God was pleased with Solomon, and the rest, as they say, is history. Solomon became renowned for his jaw-dropping wisdom. The narrative of 1 Kings from chapter 3 through chapter 7 illustrates the great wisdom of Solomon. The centerpiece of Solomon's wisdom, however, was the record of how he used delegation to govern the newly restructured districts of Israel. He put a structure in place and chose responsible people to govern under him. That is wise leadership.

You cannot delegate responsibility without also giving people authority to do the task. Oversee it, but let it go. This is where those who like to micromanage get into trouble. Some leaders simply can't seem to let go of things and give others the authority to do what is necessary. If Joshua had tried to micromanage the plan for Israel, they would never have been able to do what God commanded them to do, which was to cross over the Jordan in three days. Without proper administration and delegation, it would have taken three days just to communicate the message to the people.

Do you remember the wise advice Moses' father-in-law gave to him (Exodus 18:13–27)? Jethro saw Moses judging the people all by himself, and Jethro said, "Moses, you can't keep doing that. No man can bear this burden by himself. Get some good, faithful men. Look for men who fear God. Look for men who love truth. Look for men who hate dishonesty." Note that there's no reference to their educational background. They just needed to be men who feared God, loved truth, and couldn't be bribed.

Jethro urged Moses to develop an administrative structure and delegate both responsibility and authority, and Moses did exactly that.

Principle #3—A Leader Must Have a Plan and Clearly Communicate that Plan

A leader must have a plan, and he has to communicate that plan clearly. You have to communicate not just with words, but also with your spirit, enthusiasm, body language, and attitude. Once when I was visiting London, I had the privilege to worship at the Metropolitan Tabernacle, where the great preacher Charles Spurgeon once pastored. He is still known as "The Prince of Preachers." He was a great leader and communicator. His sermons are still widely read, even though he passed away in 1892. The church is now pastored by Peter Masters, who is also a wonderful preacher and leader.

After the service, Dr. Masters invited me back to the parlor for fellowship. There, to my amazement, was the original pulpit Spurgeon used when he was a preacher. It wasn't big and bulky like many pulpits today, but rather light and small, with wheels on the bottom. Dr. Masters explained to me that when Spurgeon preached, he would move the pulpit to his left-hand side so that the congregation could see his whole body. Spurgeon believed the art of effective and clear communication involved the entire person—not just words, but also body language, passion, and simplicity.

Communicate clearly. Notice what the plan was in Joshua 1:11, beginning with "prepare you victuals"—that is, get some food ready because the manna is about to stop. The three-point outline Joshua preached was: prepare, pass over, and possess. The plan was simple, and it could be understood by all. Many times, leaders try to sound too intelligent. They try to impress instead of express. Don't try to impress people with oratory; simply tell them the plan. Good leaders know how to meet people where they are and bring them along. This is especially true in communication. If no one can understand you, then nothing will be accomplished. It's like the old saying goes: "Just because the water is muddy doesn't mean it's deep."

Communicate with urgency. Joshua's obedience was immediate. Once he knew what God wanted, there was no waiting around. Much of God's work is accomplished in God's timing, and this was the time. He said, "This is what we're going to do—now." Joshua, no doubt, remembered what took place forty years earlier when God gave the Israelites the opportunity to cross over the Jordan, and the people hesitated because of unbelief. Numbers 14 records that the day after the children of Israel hesitated, they were ready to go over, but it was too late. God shut the door and didn't allow them to enter the land.

When God says, "Go forward," we dare not linger. A. W. Pink wrote, "There is an old adage, 'Strike while the iron is hot': act at once in response to the convictions of conscience or the promptings of the Spirit. ... Delay itself is disobedience. ... Procrastination evidences a lack of heart for the Divine precepts and an absence of concern for the Divine glory."[22]

Communicate with authority. Joshua got his orders from God. He didn't take a vote on it. When God has already said what to do, you just need to move. Besides, Joshua remembered the last time Israel voted about entering the promised land. A million said no, and two men said, "Yes, let's go." The majority is not always right, and the church is not a democracy, even though the church may sometimes use a democratic process. The church is a theocracy. God is over His church.

There are times when God makes His will clear through the leadership He has providentially put in place. When that happens, God's people simply need to submit to and follow their leaders. When "Joshua commanded the officers of the people" (Joshua 1:10), he wasn't acting as an autocrat or a tyrant. A. W. Pink wrote, "As the servant of Jehovah he was himself subject to the will of his Master, but as the leader of God's people it was both meet and necessary that he should exercise his power and control over them. Therein he has left an example which each genuine minister of the Gospel would do well to emulate."[23]

Communicate with certainty. Joshua said, "...*ye shall pass over*" (Joshua 1:11, emphasis added). He didn't wonder if they would make it. He was supremely confident because he knew this was the will of God. A leader is someone who knows where he is going and brings others with him. Confidence breeds company!

Principle #4—A Leader Has to Be Willing to Tackle Problems Head-On

Joshua 1:12–15 relates a potential problem Joshua had to deal with before things went any further. Even as he told his officers to get the people ready to cross the Jordan, Joshua personally went to the tribe of Reuben, the tribe of Gad, and the half-tribe of Manasseh. Years before, these tribes told Moses that they liked the land on that side of the Jordan and didn't want to cross over. Moses agreed that they could settle there, but he made them promise that their mighty men and soldiers would join the other tribes in fighting for the promised land. They couldn't just stay behind and let everyone else do all the fighting. The tribes of Reuben, Gad, and Manasseh agreed. Moses said, "You'd better make sure you do it because if you don't do it, your sin will find you out" (Numbers 32:23, paraphrased).

After Moses died, Joshua knew the commitment they made to Moses could easily be forgotten. He tackled the potential problem head-on. As a wise leader, Joshua knew that people don't normally do what is expected, but rather what is inspected. That's exactly what every leader should do.

You must be willing to do the difficult things. You are vulnerable and may be attacked. You must be willing to take tough stands, even if it brings criticism. There's a price to pay for leadership. Everyone wants to be liked, but leaders realize they will not always be liked. Leadership can be lonely and stressful at times.

Ted Engstrom wrote, "True leadership, even when it is

practiced by the most mature and emotionally stable person, always exacts a toll on the individual ... [so] the greater the achievement, the higher the price to be paid."[24]

Jesus, the Godliest Leader

Nobody exemplifies these principles of leadership better than the Lord Jesus Himself. Jesus got all His orders from God the Father. He gathered twelve men around Him, duplicating Himself, and duplicating them in turn. Then He delegated to them. He said, "Take this gospel into all the world" (Mark 16:15, paraphrased). He gave them authority to do it, and He dedicated them to God. In Matthew 28:19–20, Jesus clearly communicated the plan for them to follow and for us to follow. Jesus came into this world and confronted the sin problem head-on. He lived a sinless life and became a sacrifice for sin.

E. Stanley Jones told of a missionary who lost his way in an African jungle. He could find no landmarks, and the trail vanished. Eventually, stumbling upon a small hut, he asked the native living there if he could lead him out. The native nodded. Rising to his feet, he walked directly into the bush. The missionary followed on his heels. For more than an hour, they hacked their way through a dense wall of vines and grasses. The missionary became worried. "Are you sure this is the way?" he asked. "I don't see any path."

The African chuckled and said over his shoulder, "Bwana, in this place, there is no path. I am the path."[25]

Jesus blazed a trail to heaven for us. He said, "I am the way, the truth, and the life: no man cometh unto the

Father, but by me" (John 14:6). He made it clear that there was no other way. The greatest leader came into this world and taught us all how to lead.

People Who Follow a Godly Leader

And they answered Joshua, saying, All that thou command-est us we will do, and whithersoever thou sendest us, we will go.

—Joshua 1:16

These people were an encouragement to Joshua. This is a different generation from the one Moses led across the desert. As a result of their unbelief, the previous generation died in the wilderness, but this new generation responded in a different way.

Not everyone follows godly leadership. If you look in the Bible, you will see many instances of resistance. Moses had to deal with masses of ever-complaining Jews in the wilderness. Jeremiah was called the "weeping prophet" because he grieved over the rebellion of the people of Judah. Jesus faced hostility throughout His whole earthly ministry. People lied and conspired against Him. Jesus was constantly under attack and challenged.

As Moses' right-hand man for forty years, Joshua was certainly well trained, and it was very clear that he was anointed by God and promised success. Still, he couldn't do it alone. What kind of people would he need to galvanize a disciplined army at the same time as meeting the needs of such a vast crowd in tents?

People who understand unity. In any great venture, people must be unified, as the Israelites were. A people sanctified and unified is a mighty force in God's hand, while Satan's scheme is to divide and conquer.

And Joshua rose early in the morning; and they removed from Shittim, and came to Jordan, he and all the children of Israel, and lodged there before they passed over.
—Joshua 3:1

Notice where it refers to "*all* the children of Israel" (Joshua 3:1, emphasis added). The concept of unity is emphasized in variations on the phrase "all Israel," which occur throughout the book (Joshua 3:1, 7; 4:1, 14; 7:23, 25; 8:24).

I love *Peanuts* cartoons. They put things so concisely. One time, Linus was watching TV, and Lucy said, "Turn the channel."

Linus refused, saying, "Are you kidding? What makes you think you can just walk right in here and take over?"

Lucy said, "These five fingers ... individually they're nothing, but when I curl them together like this into a single unit, they form a weapon that is terrible to behold!"

"What channel do you want?" Linus said.[26]

Like Lucy's fist, when God's people come together in unity, they become a mighty force. God is glorified, sinners are justified, and the church is edified.

People who understand loyalty. These people pledged their loyalty to Joshua: "According as we hearkened unto Moses in all things, so will we hearken unto thee" (Joshua

1:17). They pledged their loyalty, but this wasn't a blind loyalty. They said, "As long as you are following the Lord the way Moses followed the Lord, then we'll follow you."

I urge you to listen to what I say, think about it, and then check it out in Scripture to make sure that what I am saying is right. If it's right, biblical, and scriptural, then you do it. Some people blindly swallow whatever they hear. They are easily deceived. God doesn't want that kind of following. The Israelites understood true loyalty. As long as Joshua followed the Lord the way Moses did, they would follow Joshua. Loyalty in Scripture is never blind. It is discerning. All leadership should be evaluated by God's Word.

Paul applauded the Bereans for checking out his teaching:

> These [the Bereans] were more noble than those in Thessalonica, in that they received the word with all readiness of mind, and searched the scriptures daily, whether those things were so.
> —*Acts 17:11*

Paul likewise told the Corinthians, "Be ye followers of me, even as I also am of Christ" (1 Corinthians 11:1).

Loyalty is never blind. Loyalty in the Scriptures is following God's servant as he follows the Lord and His Word. Don't give your loyalty to someone who just sounds good. Blind loyalty leads people to follow cult leaders like Jim Jones and David Koresh. A leader's actions and lifestyle must also align with Scripture. Jesus said, "...by their fruits ye shall know them" (Matthew 7:20).

People who understand authority. Joshua 1:18 says, "Whosoever he be that doth rebel against thy command-ment, and will not hearken unto thy words in all that thou commandest him, he shall be put to death: only be strong and of a good courage." The death sentence sounds harsh, but the people understood that Joshua was the Lord's man and was following the Lord. As long as Joshua was fol-lowing the Lord, the commands he gave were the commands of God, like those of the Old Testament proph-ets who came later. He was God's prophet, and to rebel against him was ultimately to rebel against the Lord!

We don't have prophets and apostles today the way they did in the Bible. We have preachers who are commit-ted to the Word of God. My authority comes from preaching the Bible. I stand behind His Word and tell you what God says. As long as I am faithful to tell you what the Lord says, I am speaking with the Lord's authority. That's why I say, "Check it out for yourself. Don't just believe me."

We have already mentioned that no one models the principles of leadership we see in this narrative better than Jesus does. Everyone needs to recognize this and follow Him. Like Joshua, Jesus is commanding people today to recognize His authority and unite behind Him, pledging their utmost loyalty. He doesn't ask for blind faith. He simply invites you to test His authority to see if He is in-deed from God.

Once the Jews said to Jesus, "If you are the Christ, tell

us plainly" (John 10:24 ESV). Jesus responded, "I told you, and you do not believe. The works that I do in my Father's name bear witness about me" (John 10:25 ESV). In essence, Jesus was inviting these doubters to examine the evidence for themselves. The Bible provides sufficient evidence to any honest seeker that Jesus is all that He claims to be. He is God's anointed Messiah and Savior. Since that is true, the only right response is to recognize His authority, repent, and follow Him with every ounce of loyalty in your heart.

WORKBOOK

Chapter Two Questions

Question: Where have you seen decline or damage in a family, a church, or a community because of a lack of leadership or the wrong sort of leadership? When have you seen a wise leader turn a difficult situation around for the mutual good of everyone?

_____

_____

_____

_____

_____

_____

_____

_____

_____

Question: Do you have trouble delegating? If so, why do you think that is? What qualities should you be looking for in the people to whom you delegate, and what should you do if you can't find anyone with those traits?

_____

_____

_____

_____

_____

_____

_____

_____

_____

_____

Journal: Evaluate the leaders* to whom you are loyal. Is there anyone besides Christ to whom you give blind and unquestioning loyalty? If so, ask Him to break the stronghold that person has over your life and to help you discern his or her leadership through the lens of His truth. Conversely, how are you exercising loyalty to leaders who are following God and His Word? How are you supporting them when they have to delegate tasks, confront sin, and communicate hard truths?

(*For situations involving ungodly government leaders or difficult employers, see the principles in Romans 13 and 1 Peter 2.)

_____

_____

_____

_____

_____

_____

_____

_____

_____

_____

Action: Read a book or listen to a podcast series on communication in leadership. Ask God to reveal to you how you can grow into a stronger leader who communicates correctly in whatever sphere(s) you find yourself (e.g. leading a family, a business, or a small group at church).

Chapter Two Notes

CHAPTER THREE

Genuine Faith in a Godless Place
Joshua 2:1–24

Big Idea: God delights in displaying genuine faith
in unlikely places with unlikely people to affirm His
providential work and to strengthen His people.

Once a pastor was visiting one of his church members
who worked at a local coal mine. Standing at the mouth
of the cave, he noticed a beautiful white, glowing flower.
It was growing out of the blackest and dirtiest soil. He was
captivated by the flower and wondered how a beautiful
white flower could grow in a place of such black soot and
dirt. Walking over to the flower, he reached down, gathered in his hand some coal dust, and sprinkled it on the
petals. The dust simply slid off the petals without staining
them. *"What a portrayal of a Christian!"* he thought.

The faith of believers should cause them to stand apart
from the sin and corruption of the world. The Bible says
in 1 John 5:4, "For whatsoever is born of God overcometh

the world: and this is the victory that overcometh the world, even our faith." This story is about the beautiful white flower of faith growing in a dirty, corrupt, sinful environment.

We are people of faith. Because of our faith, we should stand out against the backdrop of a corrupt and sinful world. It is our faith that gives us victory over the world.

Rahab's life is a picture of faith where we might least expect it. Why is her story here? It isn't really necessary to the theme of Joshua, the conquest of the promised land. You could take chapter 2 out of the book of Joshua, and the overall message wouldn't change. In chapter 1, the Israelites prepared to cross the Jordan, and in chapter 3, they crossed. Rahab is a bridge of faith between the two chapters. Her story is here because God wants us to see what real faith looks like and how one life can affect the history of a whole nation.

Jericho was an unlikely place to find a gentile harlot who would aid the Israelites in their quest. Jericho was the most sinful, corrupt city in a corrupt land called Canaan. Jericho was also strategic because it was first on the list of cities that Joshua had to conquer. Once he prevailed over this military stronghold, he would have access to the land north and south of it. He already knew the Lord had given him Jericho, but he was a good general and wanted to learn about the city, so he sent spies.

And Joshua the son of Nun sent out of Shittim two men to spy secretly, saying, Go view the land, even Jericho. And they went, and came into an harlot's house, named Rahab, and lodged there. And it was told the king of Jericho, saying, Behold, there came men in hither to night of the

children of Israel to search out the country. And the king
of Jericho sent unto Rahab, saying, Bring forth the men
that are come to thee, which are entered into thine house:
for they be come to search out all the country.
—Joshua 2:1–3

Rahab's Genuine Faith

Rahab is introduced to us in Joshua 2:1, where it says
that the Israelite spies went to the house of a harlot named
Rahab and lodged there. Oftentimes in Scripture, God
spotlights someone who exercised faith in a way we
wouldn't expect. Here was a gentile woman living in a
godless city who believed in the living God and was willing to risk her life for His people. It was no accident that
the spies happened to go to her place of all places. There
was only one person of faith in all of Jericho, and these
spies happened to meet her. We see here the providence
of God as He promised. What a wonderful and faithful
God we serve!

Genuine Faith Is Often Displayed Courageously

Rahab was a depraved sinner. The Bible says in Joshua
2:1 that the spies "came into an harlot's house." Some
have said that she was really an innkeeper because the
word in Hebrew can mean someone who keeps an inn.
However, James 2:25 and Hebrews 11:31 use a Greek
word for *harlot* that has a singular meaning. Rahab's
house was right on the wall of the city, which covered a
total of eight or nine acres. Archaeological evidence from
this period reveals cities with a continuous band of

connected houses lining their outer walls or embankments, just as described in Scripture.[27]

Rahab was an Amorite. The Amorites were a corrupt and vile people who even sacrificed their own children to idols. Rahab's city had already been condemned by God; it was just a matter of time before this sentence of death would be executed. Everything and everyone in the city would be destroyed (Joshua 6:21), whether the Amorites felt condemned or not! This means Rahab was also a condemned woman.

Somehow the king of Jericho found out about the two spies in the house of Rahab, and he sent some messengers. If Rahab handed them over, she would more than likely have received a reward. If she refused to hand them over or she protected them, she would be doing so at her own peril. She was risking her life. On the surface, it looked like she had nothing to gain and everything to lose by helping the spies. As theologian James Montgomery Boice explained, "Jericho was not a nice place. It was actually something of a military outpost, and we are not wrong to think that Rahab's life would not have been worth a wooden shekel if her deception had been discovered."[28]

Verses 4 through 6 of Joshua 2 show us that Rahab was resourceful as well as courageous. She hid the spies on her flat roof under some stacks of flax left there to dry. She told the king's men that the spies were gone, that they had come there but had already left.

Rahab somehow understood what was going on. She believed in God, and she believed that these men were from God, that they were servants of the Most High God, the God of Israel, the God she had come to know.

Genuine Faith Is Declared Confidently

Rahab heard the Word. Her house was an inn, and many travelers would come through there. Boice wrote, "Her home would have been a place of great gossip as strangers from near and far reported tales of foreign wonders."[29]

She told the spies, "For we have heard how the LORD dried up the water of the Red sea for you, when ye came out of Egypt; and what ye did unto the two kings of the Amorites, that were on the other side Jordan, Sihon and Og, whom ye utterly destroyed" (Joshua 2:10).

Sometimes God will use the strangest instruments to communicate His Word to people. He will use even the most crooked people. Rahab listened, and she heard the stories of God's mighty acts. The first step of faith is hearing the Word of God. True biblical faith is rooted in the Word of God!

Rahab heard the Word of God, and then she believed. She said, "And as soon as we had heard these things, our hearts did melt" (Joshua 2:11). She didn't just listen with her ears. She listened with her heart, and she believed.

Rahab confessed the Word. She said, "I know that the LORD hath given you the land" (Joshua 2:9). She verbalized what God had told Joshua: "Every place that the sole of your foot shall tread upon, that have I given unto you" (Joshua 1:3). She repeated God's promise with great confidence. God used her to confirm His promise to Joshua and the people of Israel in case there was any doubt.

Some people today find fault with the fact that Rahab lied to the king. Perhaps Rahab could have said something different without actually lying. There are pages and pages of material written on the lie of Rahab. I get asked a lot about the ethics of Rahab's lie. Is it right that she lied, or is it wrong? Was Rahab justified in telling this bold-faced lie?

There's no way around it. She did lie to these men. Is this the Bible's answer to the question that Corrie ten Boom faced when she was hiding Jews in her home? [30] She hid some Jews in the attic, and the Nazis were at the door, asking, "Do you have any Jews?" Was she supposed to say yes and live the rest of her life with the knowledge that she turned them in and sealed their deaths? Or was it excusable for her to lie about it and say no with the confidence that God understood? What was she supposed to do?

I like what Wiersbe wrote about this: "Perhaps we're expecting too much from a new believer whose knowledge of God was adequate for salvation but certainly limited when it came to the practical things of life."[31] That's not to excuse lying. It simply takes her circumstances into consideration.

Let's be honest. If we were in the same situation, wouldn't we hesitate to tell the truth? Some of us would. Remember that it was wartime in this story. Many people throughout history have been honored for deceiving the enemy at wartime. They have even been given medals for it. All of these ethical issues aside, the main lesson here is about Rahab's faith, and her faith was displayed courageously because she was willing to risk her life. True faith is willing to take a risk. Several other people used by God also found themselves fibbing for the sake of protection (Genesis 12:10–20; 20:1–18; 26:6–11; 1 Samuel 21:2), so I think we shouldn't be too hard on Rahab.

No matter where you come down on this issue, while God never condoned her lie, He *did* reward her faith. James 2:25 says that Rahab received the spies and then "sent them out another way." It never even mentions the lie. In my own faith, I find there is often some type of sin or corruption mingled in with it. I would say that none of us has ever exercised perfect faith without some degree of selfishness, sinfulness, or corruption, even in our best acts. I am like the man who said, "Lord, I believe; help thou mine unbelief" (Mark 9:24). God is gracious and kind, and He accepts my faith, though I am a sinner. He looks at the faith I do have, and He honors that faith. This is what God does for me. This is what God does for you. And this is what God did for Rahab.

Faith is grounded in the Word of God, not the words of men. Faith is boldly repeating what God has already said. This is what Rahab did. She believed, and that's why she didn't perish with those who did not believe.

Rahab turned to God from idol worship:

And as soon as we had heard these things, our hearts did melt, neither did there remain any more courage in any man, because of you: for the LORD your God, he is God in heaven above, and in earth beneath.
—Joshua 2:11

This is a monumental confession of faith. I think this is one of the most remarkable statements from the mouth of a foreigner, a gentile, in all of the Old Testament. Rahab was saying, "Your God is sovereign over all."

Canaanites believed there were gods to control different parts of the cosmos. We see this in the Old Testament, and it's also clear from extra-biblical sources, such as Canaanite religious texts.[323334] They believed there was a god who controlled the heavens. There was a god who controlled the earth, the plains. There was a god underneath the earth and gods of the water and sea, gods of the mountains, gods of the seasons of the year.

The god they believed controlled the heavens happened to be named *Baal*. He controlled the rain and thunder. He was the god of the storms. Statues of Baal depicted him with lightning bolts in his hands. In Canaanite texts, he was called "the rider of the clouds."

Canaanite religion was tied into the seasons of the year and thus with agriculture. There were two seasons: the wet season and the dry season. Their belief in their gods was tied into the weather patterns and the seasons. When it was a dry season, Baal was supposedly dead. They believed he came to life during the rainy season because when it was raining, he was on the throne.

Supposedly Baal went into the underworld and challenged Mot, the god of death and the earth beneath, and lost. His wife, Anat, would go get him and bring him back to life. This was a constant cycle called the "Baal cycle." He was warring against Yamm, the god of the seas. He was warring against Mot.

But Rahab was saying, "None of that is true. Your God

is the God of heaven above and the earth beneath. He is the only God. There are no other gods." She wasn't holding on to the gods of the Canaanites with one hand and the God of the Hebrews with the other. There are some people who come to Jesus Christ and want to hold on to the world with one hand and Jesus with the other. That's not real faith. Real faith in Jesus Christ gets rid of all idols and has allegiance to Jesus Christ alone.

Genuine Faith Is Always Demonstrated Concretely

Rahab's works revealed that her faith was real. This is why in the New Testament, James reached all the way back to the Old Testament when he wanted to give an illustration of what real faith looks like. He used Rahab as an example, referring to her works:

> *Likewise also was not Rahab the harlot justified by works, when she had received the messengers, and had sent them out another way?*
> *—James 2:25*

Someone might respond, "Wait a minute, didn't Paul say we are justified by faith?" Yet here, James said Rahab was justified by works.

It seems like Paul and James were having an argument. Some doubters and skeptics look at this and say, "Aha, here is a contradiction!" But they are wrong. Paul did say that we are justified by faith (Romans 3:21–5:2), but there is no contradiction. It's heads and tails of the same truth. The key to understanding this apparent contradiction is seeing that Paul was talking about justification before God while James was talking about justification before men. It's your works that men see: "...for man looks at the outward appearance, but the LORD looks at the heart" (1 Samuel 16:7 NKJV).

I am saved, but if you look at me, you can't see into my heart. You can't see my faith. All you can see are my works that demonstrate my real faith in God. Salvation is not by faith *plus* works, but it is by a faith that *produces* works. Paul was talking about the root of salvation, and James was talking about the fruit of salvation. There are many people who claim to know God with their mouths, but their works don't back it up. That's what James was taking aim at here. He was tackling a problem in the early church that we still have today. Many were professing to be saved, but their lives didn't show it.

The Elements of Faith

Systematic theology has traditionally recognized three elements to saving faith, which include the mind, the heart, and the will. There's an intellectual element of faith, an emotional element, and a volitional element. The word *volitional* means "the act of using one's will."[35] Another way to categorize these three elements would be: *notitia*, which means believing the facts intellectually; *assensus*, which is believing in the heart, a conviction that it is true; and *fiducia*, a commitment of the will.[36] Wiersbe wrote, "Martyn Lloyd-Jones reminds us, 'Faith shows itself in the whole personality.' True saving faith isn't just a feat of intellectual gymnastics by which we convince ourselves that something is true that really isn't true."[37]

In the book of James, James described dead faith: "Even so faith, if it hath not works, is dead, being alone" (James 2:17). That is, dead faith is faith that involves only the mind. There are many people today who say that they believe in Jesus. If you were to ask them if they believe that Jesus is the risen Son of God, they would say, "Yes!" But that doesn't mean they possess saving faith. They have an intellectual understanding of the doctrinal facts about Christ, but it goes no further than that. That kind of faith, as James described it, is "alone." It's nothing more than a mental acknowledgement. There are many people today who think that kind of faith is all that is necessary, but James asked the rhetorical question, "Can [that kind of] faith save him?" (James 2:14). The obvious answer is no.

James also addressed demonic faith: "Thou believest that there is one God; thou doest well: the devils also believe, and tremble" (James 2:19). James seems to have been a bit sarcastic here as he dealt with the idea of emotions and genuine faith. To paraphrase, he was saying, "You believe in one God. Well, good for you, but even demons believe that."

Here James was referring to the Jewish confession in Deuteronomy known as "the Shema." This is considered an orthodox confession. James was saying, "You are orthodox in your belief, and that is all good and fine, but so are the demons. And they take it one step further. They tremble at the idea of God." Demons have an emotional response to what they believe, but no demon is saved. That's demonic faith. There are some people who base their salvation on an emotional decision they made one time in church when their hearts were stirred, perhaps about an orthodox teaching they heard. They might have wept or approached an altar with tears, yet when they left church, they were the same people. Nothing about their lives was different. That is demonic faith, and it, too, comes short of genuine, saving faith.

Then there's true faith: "Seest thou how faith wrought with his works, and by works was faith made perfect?" (James 2:22). In other words, faith was made mature or complete by works. This is what we can call *dynamic faith*. It's accompanied by a commitment of the will. To further illustrate dynamic faith, let's say that one day a man decides to go see his doctor. While he is in the waiting room, he reaches down and grabs a magazine and begins to read an article about the danger of smoking. It's a very well-written and persuasive piece, complete with statistics about cancer and lung disease. After reading the article, the man is fully convinced that everything written in it is absolutely true. Still, after he leaves the doctor's office, he lights up a cigarette and smokes. Nothing about the article changes his behavior.

He returns to the doctor's office on another day, and while in the waiting room, he again reads the same article. This time, not only is he convinced of the truth of it, but he begins to cry. The thought of dying of cancer and leaving his family behind stirs his emotions, yet he reaches into his pocket, pulls out a cigarette, and lights up. What kind of faith is that? It is demonic faith. It has intellectual and emotional elements, but nothing more.

Yet again, this man returns to the same doctor's office

and reads the same article, but with a different outcome. This time, after reading the article and believing every word of it and being stirred in his heart, he reaches into his pocket, pulls out his package of cigarettes, crumples them up, and throws them in the trash can. He then stands up and says, "I will never smoke again." What kind of faith is that? It's dynamic faith because it includes not just the intellectual and emotional elements, but also the volitional element. It's made complete by the commitment of the will. This is what James was saying about genuine, saving faith.

When all three elements are applied to the Word of God, the result is salvation. The Bible illustrates many who exercised this quality of faith. For example, "By faith Noah, being warned of God of things not seen as yet [the intellect], moved with fear [the emotions], prepared an ark [the will] to the saving of his house" (Hebrews 11:7). Rahab's experience was similar to that of Noah.

Rahab's Faith in Action

Rahab had dynamic faith. She believed, and she made a commitment to God to act. That's true faith. She risked her life by receiving the spies and also by sending them out another way.

Once when the great tightrope walker Charles Blondin was performing on a cable across Niagara Falls, he asked his audience, "How many of you believe I can walk across that wire, pushing a wheelbarrow?" The people all cheered, and he then asked, "How many of you think I can do it with a man in the wheelbarrow?"

As his audience cheered again, Blondin pointed to one man who cheered more enthusiastically than everyone else. Blondin pointed to that man and said, "You are my man. Get in the wheelbarrow." The man's face turned pale. He spun around on his heels and escaped rapidly. He believed in Blondin's ability, but he wasn't ready to make a commitment. This man wasn't ready to risk his life to prove his belief,[38] but Rahab got into the wheelbarrow!

When a person truly calls upon Christ and comes to faith, the first thing that person thinks about is his or her family and others. That's what Rahab did.

> Now therefore, I pray you, swear unto me by the LORD, since I have shewed you kindness, that ye will also shew kindness unto my father's house, and give me a true token: And that ye will save alive my father, and my mother, and my brethren, and my sisters, and all that they have, and deliver our lives from death.
> —*Joshua 2:12–13*

She wanted *all* of her family safe.

The spies said, "Leave this scarlet cord that you're going to use to let us out hanging in your window, and this will be a safe house for whomever is inside. When we come and we see this scarlet cord hanging in the window, judgment will pass over this house" (Joshua 2:18, paraphrased).

Does this remind you of the blood of Passover? And whom does the blood of Passover remind us of? The blood of the Lord, Jesus Christ. Again, the New Testament is revealed in the Old.

We see the blood of Christ in a typical way, and all those who are under the blood will be safe from the judgment. Rahab received the grace she asked for, and the rest of her family did as well.

The spies left and returned to Joshua. They told him all about Rahab. Rahab had convinced them of her faith and her commitment to God's purposes. They said to Joshua, "Truly the LORD hath delivered into our hands all the land; for even all the inhabitants of the country do faint because of us" (Joshua 2:24).

Rahab became part of the nation of Israel. She married a Jewish man named Salmon. They had a son named Boaz. Boaz married Ruth. They had a son named Obed, who was the father of Jesse, who was the father of David (Matthew 1:5–6). So, we see Rahab in the lineage of the Lord Jesus Christ in the New Testament. She became the great-great-great-great-(etc.)grandmother of Jesus. Talk about victorious faith that overcomes the world!

Do you want God to do great things for you? It's according to your faith. We weren't born with any special spiritual privileges. Unlike the Israelites, but like Rahab, we were outside the covenant and had to come to God by faith. It doesn't matter who you are—your race, face, or place. If you come to God desiring and seeking His mercy, you will receive it. You will be forgiven for your sin and adopted into the family of God. Hallelujah!

Chapter Three Questions

Question: What are some idols you turned from when you came to Christ? In what ways have you tried to hold on to the world and to Christ at the same time? What happens when a person does this, and what does the Bible say about it (see James 4:1–6 and Luke 16:13)?

_____

_____

_____

_____

_____

_____

_____

_____

_____

Question: How has your faith in God been demonstrated and displayed by your works? What do your lifestyle and decisions tell others about your inner beliefs and affections?

_____

_____

_____

_____

_____

_____

_____

_____

_____

Journal: How has faith in Jesus Christ changed your life? In what ways were you an unlikely candidate to become a man or woman of faith? How has God rewarded your small acts of obedient faith with a greater place and ministry in His kingdom?

_____

_____

_____

_____

_____

_____

_____

_____

_____

Action: Read chapter 11 of Hebrews. Write out what each person _believed_ about God and how he or she _acted_ upon that belief.

Chapter Three Notes

CHAPTER FOUR

Crossing Impossible Rivers
Joshua 3:1–17

Big Idea: *God is willing and able to help you cross the impossible rivers of life you will face as you seek to do His will if you are willing to get your feet wet in faith.*

Their camp must have stretched for miles. It took the officers three days to pass through and tell everyone the plan (Joshua 3:2). Time to pack up and get ready to move. The Jordan was flooded. Humanly speaking, this was the worst time to cross. Scripture doesn't record any dissent, but surely some had to wonder what Joshua was thinking. What about the mud, the current, the deep water? Could the children and animals possibly make it? If they waited a couple of weeks for the water to go down, it would be a piece of cake.

Normally, the Jordan River was about a hundred feet wide at Gilgal.[39] There were certain times of the year, however, when the river was wider than normal. They came to the Jordan during the flood season, when the river would normally overflow its banks. What was normally a quiet, soft-flowing river became a raging torrent. The spring rains along with the melting snows from the Lebanon mountains flowed into it, swelling the banks. The prophet Jeremiah referred to this as "the swelling of Jordan" (Jeremiah 12:5). Why cross now? What was the hurry?

Doubtless their parents had told them about crossing the Red Sea, but that was then. The Egyptians were bearing down on the Israelites at the Red Sea. They were fleeing for their lives. There wasn't anyone chasing them now, and Moses was dead. Did God *really* tell Joshua they should risk their lives and cross that angry river?

God had promised Joshua that He would be with him: "This day will I begin to magnify thee in the sight of all Israel, that they may know that, as I was with Moses, so I will be with thee" (Joshua 3:7). He was about to affirm His power and His presence for all the people to see so they wouldn't question Joshua's leadership again. God uses people to accomplish His purposes. Only God can exalt and establish His leaders in the hearts of people. If people seek to exalt themselves, they will fail. If Joshua had tried to magnify himself, he would have fallen on his face! God had the perfect plan to exalt him.

Timing Is Everything

Even though it may not seem like it to us, God's timing is always right. God may set before you an insurmountable challenge at what seems like the worst possible time in your season of life. Solomon reminded us, "To every thing there is a season, and a time to every purpose under the heaven" (Ecclesiastes 3:1). Remember that God is providentially working out His purpose for a specific reason that sometimes may be hidden from us. There are no accidents, only acts of providence. Through Scripture, we can discern some general reasons why God would bring us to impossible rivers in our lives.

God wants to demonstrate His supernatural power. God does things in such a way that no man can boast. No one could have stopped the cascading river but God. They had to depend totally and completely upon Him for His power. God also wants to demonstrate His power for you, in you, and through you. God delights in doing that. Charles Spurgeon said, "God does not want your strength, He has more than enough of that. He wants your weakness."[40] When we give God our weakness and become fully dependent on His power, we are at the place where God will do wonders for us.

God always wants to stretch the faith of His people. God could easily have had them cross the Jordan during the dry season. That was something they could have handled on their own, but it wouldn't have tested their faith. The Israelites faced an insurmountable problem, and God wanted to see how they would respond. Sometimes as a believer, your first response to difficulty may be to doubt God, maybe even to complain, but He wants to stretch your faith. He wants to develop your spiritual strength and understanding.

The men and women we read about in Scripture had this is common. God would bring them through a series of tests to strengthen their faith and dependence on Him. Abraham went through a series of tests that strengthened his faith to the point where he "staggered not at the promise of God" (Romans 4:20). Before David became king, he endured a series of tests that made him a man after God's own heart (Acts 13:22). God still works the same way in the lives of His people today. If God has placed an impossible river in front of you, it's because He has some important task for you on the other side.

They were going somewhere they had never been before, and they needed God to lead them. Joshua said to the people, "...you have not passed this way before" (Joshua 3:4 ESV). God doesn't always do the same thing the same way. When God parted the water for Moses, He had Moses stretch out his rod (Exodus 14). When God parted the waters for Elijah and Elisha, He had them strike the waters with a mantle, or cloak (2 Kings 2). God did something completely different for Joshua. It's usually counterproductive to model your approach after something that worked for someone else in the past. Our creative Lord wants to issue you unique orders for your situation.

God wants to get you out of your comfort zone. You will have impassible rivers of your own at times. You will go to places you have never been before on your spiritual journey. This means God wants you to trust Him. He has promised, "When thou passest through the waters, I will be with thee; and through the rivers, they shall not overflow thee: when thou walkest through the fire, thou shalt not be burned; neither shall the flame kindle upon thee" (Isaiah 43:2). Just as the Israelites recalled the stories of crossing the Red Sea, the Lord also wants you to remember His faithfulness to you in the past.

Crossing the River

The Jordan represents difficulty and challenges that you must face and overcome. It may be a river of doubt or some spiritual weakness. It may be a river of sin besetting you. It may be a river of sickness or family difficulty. We all will come to impossible rivers at some point in our lives. The question is what you will do when you face them. The book of Joshua gives clear guidelines to mark your path and make your passage easier through your own rough waters.

Sanctify Yourself

> *And Joshua said unto the people, Sanctify yourselves: for to morrow the LORD will do wonders among you.*
> *—Joshua 3:5*

Joshua wasn't exactly sure what God was going to do, but he was confident that God was going to do something great! He said to the people, "Sanctify yourselves." Joshua wanted no sin to hinder their progress. They needed the love and power of God to be fresh in their

minds. God had already told them how to sanctify themselves earlier in the journey:

> *This book of the law shall not depart out of thy mouth; but*
> *thou shalt meditate therein day and night, that thou may-*
> *est observe to do according to all that is written therein:*
> *for then thou shalt make thy way prosperous, and then*
> *thou shalt have good success.*
> —*Joshua 1:8*

In other words, leave sin behind. I believe the reason
God is not doing wonders among some Christians today
is because they are living impure lives. The weight of sin
is crippling their walk with Him.

> *Behold, the LORD's hand is not shortened, that it cannot*
> *save; neither his ear heavy, that it cannot hear: But your*
> *iniquities have separated between you and your God....*
> —*Isaiah 59:1-2*

> *If a man therefore purge himself from these, he shall be a*
> *vessel unto honour, sanctified, and meet for the master's*
> *use, and prepared unto every good work.*
> —*2 Timothy 2:21*

Expect Miracles

It's interesting to me that in the first five verses of
chapter 3, Joshua still didn't know how God was going to
get them to the other side. Joshua didn't need to come up
with the plan. He just needed to believe that God had a

glorious plan. He said to the people, "Listen, tomorrow the Lord is going to do wonders for you and among you" (Joshua 3:5, paraphrased). God is always ready to do great things on behalf of His people. God is ready to do great things on your behalf, so expect miracles.

Face the River

It doesn't help to pretend that a problem is not there. Denial just wastes precious time, keeping you bogged down in the mire. Recognize the challenge for what it is. Face it bravely and confront that river in the way God tells you, starting immediately, as Joshua did: "Joshua rose early in the morning; and they removed from Shittim, and came to Jordan" (Joshua 3:1).

Watch God

> And they [the officers] commanded the people, saying, When ye see the ark of the covenant of the LORD your God, and the priests the Levites bearing it, then ye shall remove from your place, and go after it.
> —*Joshua 3:3*

When the people saw the ark, they believed God's presence was there with them. In a sense, Joshua said that when God moved, they were to move. This is a valuable spiritual lesson. Learn to be sensitive to the movement of God around you. Ask the Holy Spirit to help you grow in your discernment. When you need a miracle, don't tell God what He needs to do. You rarely know the right answer to the problem. *Watch* and wait to see His hand at work. If you give it to Him, leave it with Him.

Follow God

The people had to go forward. It's not enough to know what God is doing. There comes a time when you must be willing to leave your comfort zone and follow Him. It may not be the easiest thing you will do, but it's always the right thing to step out in faith.

God did an incredible thing. The waters stood, rose up, and were cut off. The moment the priests put their feet in the water, it happened. The people not only crossed the river, but crossed on dry land!

God told Joshua:

> And it shall come to pass, as soon as the soles of the feet of the priests that bear the ark of the LORD, the LORD of all the earth, shall rest in the waters of Jordan, that the waters of Jordan shall be cut off from the waters that come down from above; and they shall stand upon an heap.
> —*Joshua 3:13*

The Lord of all the earth rested in the flood waters, holding them back! The Israelites could not have been safer anywhere else on earth. But first, they had to go into the water. You may want to say, "God, open up the waters, and then I'll go through the parting." You would like it all mapped out in front of you, but God doesn't operate that way. Unless you are willing to step out in faith and get your feet wet, you are not likely to make a whole lot of progress in the Christian life. The miracle of God was in response to the faith of the people, and His miracle for you will be in response to your faith.

Honor God

Yet there shall be a space between you and it, about two thousand cubits by measure: come not near unto it, that ye may know the way by which ye must go: for ye have not passed this way heretofore.

—Joshua 3:4

The space between the people and the ark was to be about 3,000 feet, or half a mile. That gap made it possible for everyone in Israel, not just the people in the front of the line, to see what was happening on the river. Let there be no mistake. God Himself, not Joshua, was leading them into the promised land, and He wanted to be sure they understood.

The gap between the people and the ark was also an expression of reverence and honor toward the ark, which represented God. They did not want to presume on His holy presence. When God leads, you should follow Him in awe and reverence.

The Impossible Made Possible

And as they that bare the ark were come unto Jordan, and the feet of the priests that bare the ark were dipped in the brim of the water, (for Jordan overfloweth all his banks all the time of harvest,)

That the waters which came down from above stood and rose up upon an heap very far from the city Adam, that is beside Zaretan: and those that came down toward the sea of the plain, even the salt sea, failed, and were cut off: and the people passed over right against Jericho.

And the priests that bare the ark of the covenant of the LORD stood firm on dry ground in the midst of Jordan, and all the Israelites passed over on dry ground, until all the people were passed clean over Jordan.

—Joshua 3:15–17

There are three verbs in this passage that describe what happened: "stood," "rose up," and "were cut off." The idea is that the flowing river stopped, and the waters stood up as a heap. The word *heap* is the same term that describes the wall of water at the Exodus crossing of the Red Sea (Exodus 15:8; Psalm 33:7). Joshua 3:16 mentions "the city Adam." This city was about sixteen miles north of the place where they crossed. This place is identified today as Tell ed-Damiyeh.[41]

Of course, skeptics and liberal scholars come along and say, "Well, this was no miracle. This was a natural phenomenon." Critical scholars point to two natural occurrences to explain away the supernatural event. On December 8, 1267, an earthquake caused the high banks of the Jordan to collapse near Tell ed-Damiyeh, damming the river for about ten hours. On July 11, 1927, another earthquake near the same location blocked the river for twenty-one hours. Donald Campbell argued:[42]

Of course, these stoppages did not occur during flood season. Admittedly God could have employed natural causes such as an earthquake and a landslide and the timing would have still made it a miraculous intervention. But does the biblical text allow for such an interpretation of this event?

Campbell also argued that several supernatural elements were involved, proving this was nothing other than a supernatural act of God:[43]

1.) This event was predicted in 3:13, 15—Joshua told them in detail what was going to happen.

2.) The timing was exact 3:15.

3.) This took place when the river was at flood stage.

4.) The wall of water was held in place for many hours, possibly the entire day.

5.) The soft wet soil became dry at once 3:17.

6.) The water returned immediately as soon as the people had crossed over and the priests came up out of the river. 4:18.

Wow, what a miracle! That's what happens when we believe in God's Word and act in faith. This is really a greater miracle than the Red Sea because when God opened the Red Sea, it was by the arm of one man whom God honored. But here, God honored the faith of a whole multitude. God will do miracles for us! He will "do exceedingly abundantly above all that we ask or think" (Ephesians 3:20 NKJV). Do you believe that?

I recently read a story about a man named George Dantzig, who was a senior at Stanford University during the

Great Depression.[44] George needed to graduate at the top of his class if he expected to get a job. Well, George was not at the top of his class. He was at the bottom. His only hope was to ace the final.

Like many of us, George thought cramming would be the ticket, but his late-night efforts made him late for class the next day. He missed the professor's instructions for taking the test. Sheepishly, George sat down and went to work.

George finished all the math problems on the exam before he dug into two problems written on the board. Then he panicked because the problems were so hard that he was sure he would fail! His only hope was to take them home to work on, if possible. Somewhat puzzled, the professor agreed.

George attacked those problems with a vengeance and handed in his paper, hoping for the best. The very next morning, there was a knock on his door. It was his professor, who informed George that he had just made mathematics history by solving problems no one else could! Because George didn't know these problems were impossible for even the greatest genius, he didn't know he couldn't solve them—so he did.

When I read that, I thought, *"God's people are people who don't know there are problems that are impossible to solve."* Do you know why? Because we serve a God of the possible, and He can do anything. We don't know a problem that's impossible to solve because we follow the powerful, living God. With Him, "all things are possible" (Matthew 19:26).

Erect a Memorial

> *And it came to pass, when all the people were clean passed over Jordan, that the LORD spake unto Joshua, saying, Take you twelve men out of the people, out of every tribe a man, And command ye them, saying, Take you hence out of the midst of Jordan, out of the place where the priests' feet stood firm, twelve stones, and ye shall carry them over with you, and leave them in the lodging place, where ye shall lodge this night.*
>
> —*Joshua 4:1–3*

We have a tendency to forget what God does. The danger is that we often forget the God who helped us. James Montgomery Boice wrote, "The people needed a memorial because, like ourselves, they tended to forget the goodness and mighty acts of God on their behalf."[45]

A memorial is a reminder to God's people. It's a reminder of a place and time when God intervened in your life and a reminder of God Himself, a thank you for His act of love.

> *"...then beware, **lest you forget** the LORD who brought you out of the land of Egypt, from the house of bondage. You shall fear the LORD your God and serve Him, and shall take oaths in His name. You shall not go after other gods, the gods of the peoples who are all around you (for the LORD your God is a jealous God among you), lest the anger of the LORD your God be aroused against you and destroy you from the face of the earth.*
>
> —**Deuteronomy 6:12–15** *(NKJV, emphasis added)*

Memorials in the Bible

Sometimes in the Bible, you will see that when God does something great, He will have His people put up a stone or a crude altar as a memorial. Noah, Abraham, Isaac, and Jacob all built stone memorials in places where they had encountered God in a special way. Now Joshua would follow their example:

> *And the children of Israel did so as Joshua commanded, and took up twelve stones out of the midst of Jordan, as the LORD spake unto Joshua, according to the number of the tribes of the children of Israel, and carried them over with them unto the place where they lodged, and laid them down there.*
>
> *—Joshua 4:8*

Joshua went another step. Not only did they put a memorial on the West Bank of the Jordan, but Joshua also put a memorial right there in the middle of the river, on the very spot where the priests stood, so the people of Israel would remember where the ark of the covenant was and what the Lord did for them (Joshua 4:9).

The memorial erected on the West Bank of the Jordan became known as Gilgal (Joshua 5:9). Gilgal comes from a word that means "a rolling thing." It has the idea of a wheel in Hebrew, but it captures the idea of rolling or rolling away.[46] The memorial was a circle of stones, and every time the people of Israel came to Gilgal, they would see that memorial and be reminded of how God rolled away the reproach of Egypt and all the other nations and did something great for His people.

Gilgal became an important place in Israel's history. Israel crowned their first king at Gilgal (1 Samuel 11:15). David stayed at Gilgal after coming back from Absalom's rebellion (2 Samuel 19:40). Samuel visited Gilgal often. Elijah and Elisha established a school of prophets at Gilgal (2 Kings 4:38–41). Whoever came to Gilgal saw this memorial and was reminded of the great things God had done for Israel.

The Gilgal Memorial of Stones

Why did the Lord want Joshua to build a memorial at Gilgal? He knew the road ahead would be hard. The Israelites had a lot of battles ahead of them. With each new battle, they could come back to look at that memorial. The stones would remind them of the power of God and that God was present with His people, clearing the way before them. He promised them, "My Presence will go with you, and I will give you rest" (Exodus 33:14 NKJV).

God's people need reminders of the power and love of the living God. We also need to remind our children. Tough times engulf every generation. Gilgal provided a memorial they could see and touch, even if they weren't there for the miracle itself. A memorial is also a testimony to unbelievers, that it may sow faith in their hearts to trust in the living God:

That all the people of the earth might know the hand of the
LORD, that it is mighty: that ye might fear the LORD your
God for ever.

—*Joshua 4:24*

Theologian Francis Schaeffer said, "The stones were
to tell the other nations round about that this God is different. He really exists; he is a living God, a God of real
power who is immanent in the world."[47]

These stones at Gilgal not only represent the presence
of God in the past, but also acknowledge a principle, a
bigger picture. Crossing the Jordan foreshadows the
death, burial, and resurrection of the Lord Jesus Christ.
The Jordan River flows down into the Dead Sea. It's a
picture of judgment and death. The ark represents the
Lord Jesus Christ. The ark went down into the Jordan, but
it came out on the other side. Even so, Jesus entered into
the glacial waters of death, but He didn't stay there. He
came out on the other side and rose from the dead.

Joshua 3:16 says that when the ark went into the water,
it stopped the flow of the Jordan all the way back to the
city of Adam, about sixteen miles north of the place where
they crossed. Because of Jesus' death, burial, and resurrection, He stopped the flow of judgment in your life all
the way back to your father Adam. He gave you eternal
victory.

The stones in the midst of the Jordan speak of your un-
ion with Christ. Because of Jesus' death and resurrection,
you have something better than the ark of the covenant!
You have the presence of God in the person of the Holy
Spirit. He indwells you, and He will go before you and

lead you safely through all your unknowns.

Memorials are not just an intellectual reminder. They are designed to stir our affections, provoke emotion, and provide inspiration. When we see a memorial to something God has done, it should stir our hearts. Every time we come to the Lord's supper, this is a memorial. We are remembering what Jesus did for us.

Memorials at Home

You should erect memorials to the acts of God in your life, just as God instructed Joshua to do after the Israelites passed through the flood waters. When you write things down, you better remember the details and feelings of victories in your life. The written account serves as a memorial. Keep a journal or a "God notebook" that you can share with your children and others when appropriate.

Do you have other memorials in your home? Memorials that others can see, that your children can see? It may be a worn-out Bible. It may be a tear-stained prayer list. Perhaps you have a scripture that means a lot to you on your wall in the form of a needlework piece or a banner. Maybe you have a hand-carved cross. The best memorial, of course, is your changed life, a life changed by the power of Almighty God.

WORKBOOK

Chapter Four Questions

Question: *God doesn't always do the same thing the same way. It's usually counterproductive to model your approach after something that worked for someone else in the past.* Describe a time when you expected God to work in your life the same way He had in someone else's. How did this expectation affect your relationship with God and your ability to understand His will? What are some things that never change about how God deals with His people, and what are some ways He demonstrates His creativity and each individual's uniqueness?

_____

_____

_____

_____

_____

_____

_____

_____

_____

_____

_____

Question: How does sin hinder God's work in a believer's life? What are some areas where you need to sanctify yourself? How can you effectively examine your own life for sinful attitudes and destructive thought patterns? What are some things that are not sin but may still be hindrances to your fellowship with God and ministry for Him? (See Hebrews 12:1.)

_____

_____

_____

_____

_____

_____

_____

_____

_____

_____

_____

Journal: What is your comfort zone? It isn't inherently bad, but it's rarely where God wants you to stay. What is one step of faith or opportunity that God has put on your heart that's far outside your comfort zone? How will you face the challenge? How will you watch, follow, and honor God as He does the impossible through you?

_____

_____

_____

_____

_____

_____

_____

_____

_____

_____

_____

Action: Look back over your spiritual journey. What events, moments of decision, victories, and moments of grace stand out to you? How can you erect "memorial stones" for these moments to remember God's work in and through your life?

Chapter Four Notes

_____

_____

_____

_____

_____

_____

_____

_____

_____

_____

_____

_____

_____

_____

_____

_____

_____

_____

_____

_____

CHAPTER FIVE

Tearing Down Strongholds
Joshua 6:1–27

Big Idea: The strongholds that stand between you and your spiritual inheritance will fall as you circle them in prayer and claim the victory provided by your Captain.

Now Jericho was straitly shut up because of the children of Israel: none went out, and none came in. And the LORD said unto Joshua, See, I have given into thine hand Jericho, and the king thereof, and the mighty men of valour.
                                                          —Joshua 6:1–2

Jericho was braced for attack. It would be hard to miss the movement of two million people coming your way across the plain. It's unlikely, however, that they were terribly worried. Their walls were formidable. Jericho was their stronghold. Archaeologist Bryant Wood wrote this about Jericho's fortification: "The mound, or 'tell' of

Jericho was surrounded by a great earthen rampart, or embankment, with a stone retaining wall at its base. The retaining wall was some four to five meters (12–15 feet) high. On top of that was a mudbrick wall two meters (six feet) thick and about six to eight meters (20–26 feet) high. At the crest of the embankment was a similar mudbrick wall whose base was roughly 14 meters (46 feet) above the ground level outside the retaining wall."[48] Who could possibly breech these walls and conquer this city? All they had to do was stay put and fight from inside.

Webster's Dictionary defines a stronghold as a place of security or survival.[49] In ancient days, nobles and nations built strongholds as a refuge from invading armies. When armies came against the stronghold, they rarely won. It took a lot of strength, skill, and wisdom to overcome the strong walls of thick, solid stones. The defending soldiers could very effectively rain down arrows from the walls onto the invading troops. Nevertheless, if the children of Israel were going to claim their Canaan, Jericho had to fall. Why?

Jericho was a sinful city. This was a wicked place. The people worshiped idols and were grossly immoral. They did incredible evil in the sight of the Lord. Some of the sins are listed in Leviticus 18, including child sacrifice. Hundreds of years earlier, God told Abraham that his descendants would be an instrument of judgment because of the iniquity of the Canaanites (Genesis 15). God declared holy war against this city and all the inhabitants of Canaan (Deuteronomy 7:2; 13:15; 20:17; Joshua 6:17–18).

Jericho was a strategic city. If Joshua and Israel could take this city, then the rest of the land of Canaan would be open and vulnerable. Joshua would have access to the whole land. The book of Joshua reveals that after Jericho fell, Joshua followed with three military campaigns: the central campaign—Ai, Bethel, Shiloh, and Shechem; the southern campaign—Gibeon, Beth-horon, Makkedah, Libnah, Lachish, Eglon, Debir, Hebron, and Jerusalem; and the northern campaign—Hazor, Merom, and Kadesh. Conquering Jericho opened the way to great victories!

Bring Down the Walls

God already had a plan for Joshua to overtake Jericho. Joshua didn't submit a plan to the Lord and say, "Here, Lord, I have a plan. Bless my plan." Instead, he said, "Lord, what do You want me, Your servant, to do?"

God's instructions didn't make a whole lot of sense. He didn't ask Joshua to dig trenches, construct towers and ramparts, or build siege ladders as they might conventionally have done. Rather, for six days, all the people were to parade around the city walls in a specific and precise order: the armed men first, then seven priests with seven trumpets, then the ark, and then all the rest of the people (Joshua 6:3–5). They marched once a day for six days. No one was to speak until Joshua commanded them to do so. After the march, they went back to camp for the night (Joshua 6:10–14).

And Joshua had commanded the people, saying, Ye shall not shout, nor make any noise with your voice, neither

*shall any word proceed out of your mouth, until the day I
bid you shout; then shall ye shout.*

—*Joshua 6:10*

God's orders are designed to test our faith. This plan
leaves us scratching our heads in wonder. You may think
you know the best way, but you don't. God wants you to
have faith in Him without question. God was going to
make sure that when this city fell, it wouldn't be by human
wisdom.

*For it is written, I will destroy the wisdom of the wise, and
will bring to nothing the understanding of the prudent.
Where is the wise? where is the scribe? where is the dis-
puter of this world? hath not God made foolish the wisdom
of this world?*

—*1 Corinthians 1:19–20*

*God's orders are sometimes designed to test our pa-
tience.* The city didn't fall overnight. It must have taken
the army quite a while to walk around it. Meanwhile, they
had to listen to all that ridicule coming from the people
inside, but they had to be patient and keep doing what God
told them to do. It might have seemed like a futile waste
of time to devote an entire week to the taking of one city.
They were armed and ready for battle. Impatience was one
of Israel's besetting sins, and God was trying to teach
them patience as well as faith.

Sometimes God's orders are designed to test our self-control. If the week's schedule was a test of their patience, the divine command of silence was a test of their self-control. They weren't allowed to say a word during that whole time—no shouting back at the catcalls, no discussing how silly it seemed, no complaining about sore feet or trying to hurry the ones in the front of the line.

Sometimes God's orders are designed to test our obedience. God wanted to see whether or not Israel would obey. Sometimes God may ask you to do something that's unreasonable or illogical just to see if you are willing to obey. General George Patton had an unusual way of selecting leaders for promotion. In the book *General Patton's Principles for Life and Leadership*, written by Porter B. Williamson, one of Patton's staff officers, he described Patton's procedure. General Patton would line up his candidates and say, "Men, I want a trench dug behind that warehouse. Dig it eight feet long and three feet wide—six inches deep."[50]

Then the general would leave the men to their work. Unknown to them, however, he would go to a room in the warehouse next to where the digging tools were kept. As the men were getting the tools to dig the trench, Patton would hear every word they said. Some complained that it was demeaning work for a lieutenant or that the trench should be dug by power equipment. Others would gripe about having to dig a stupid, pointless trench in such lousy weather. Others would argue about why the general would want a trench only six inches deep. But finally, one of the men would say, "Who cares what the General wants to do with this trench? Let's just do what we were told. Let's just dig it and get it over with!" That's the man Patton would promote. God is looking for soldiers who will follow His orders obediently and get the job done!

For years, when I read this chapter in Joshua, I thought it strange. I couldn't figure out why God would design a military strategy with such an odd plan. But one day, it finally dawned on me. This was not a military strategy. This was a dedication service. This was a religious parade, a worship service. By marching in silence, the people of Israel were actually saying, "Lord, this city belongs to You, and this ritual is a dedication service. Tearing down strongholds is not our work. As we encircle this city, we're giving this city over to You. We're giving this city into Your hands."

It Is All God's Work

And it came to pass on the seventh day, that they rose early about the dawning of the day, and compassed the city after the same manner seven times: only on that day they compassed the city seven times. And it came to pass at the seventh time, when the priests blew with the trumpets, Joshua said unto the people, Shout; for the LORD hath given you the city. ... So the people shouted when the priests blew with the trumpets: and it came to pass, when the people heard the sound of the trumpet, and the people shouted with a great shout, that the wall fell down flat, so that the people went up into the city, every man straight before him, and they took the city.

—Joshua 6:15–16, 20

A Multitude of Seven

Did you notice that while you are reading this, the number seven is all over this passage? We see seven priests, seven trumpets, seven days, seven circuits, and the seventh day.

> In biblical numerology the number seven represents completeness or perfection. The Hebrew word translated "seven" (shevah) comes from a root that means "to be full, to be satisfied." When God finished His work of creation, He rested on the seventh day and sanctified it (Genesis 2:3); and this helped give the number seven its sacred significance.
>
> The Jews noted that there were seven promises in God's covenant with Abraham (Genesis 12:1-3) and seven branches on the lampstand or candlestick in the tabernacle (Exodus 37:17-24). Anything involving the number seven was especially sacred to them. It spoke of God's ability to finish whatever He started.[51]

On the seventh day of the Israelite siege of Jericho, the city fell.

Silence

The emphasis is that this was going to be the solemn dedication. Silence even included spoken prayer. There are times in our Christian lives when we just need to be still and know that He is God (Psalm 46:10). Give that stronghold to the Lord in silent prayer, knowing that He is

God and there is no other. F.B. Meyer calls "Silence" the hardest of all commandments:[52]

> That our voice should not be heard; that no word should proceed from our mouth; that we should utter our complaints to God alone—all this is foreign to our habits and taste. As death is the last enemy to be destroyed in the universe of God, so is the restraint of the tongue that last lesson learned by his children. ... It is only the still heart that can reflect the heaven of God's overarching care, or detect the least whisper of his voice through its quiet atmosphere.

Silence and prayer require discipline, especially in an age when everyone feels that he or she should be heard. The Apostle James reminds us that the ability to control one's tongue is a mark of spiritual maturity (James 3).

Trumpets

Why the trumpets? Trumpets were used to call people together for solemn feasts and services:

> *And the LORD spake unto Moses, saying, Make thee two trumpets of silver; of a whole piece shalt thou make them: that thou mayest use them for the calling of the assembly, and for the journeying of the camps.*
> **—Numbers 10:1-2**

Trumpets were also used in warfare:

And if ye go to war in your land against the enemy that oppresseth you, then ye shall blow an alarm with the trumpets; and ye shall be remembered before the LORD your God, and ye shall be saved from your enemies.

—*Numbers 10:9*

Claimed by Faith

*So the people shouted when the priests blew with the trumpets: and it came to pass, when the people heard the sound of the trumpet, and the people **shouted** with a great shout, that the wall fell down flat, so that the people went up into the city, every man straight before him, and they took the city.*

—*Joshua 6:20 (emphasis mine)*

Why did they shout? Well, first of all, because God told them to shout. Secondly, this was a claim of faith. They claimed the promise of God. The Hebrew verb used here for *shout* can mean a shout of praise to the Lord.[53]

The word is translated sometimes as "joyful noise." Why would they make a joyful noise of praise to the Lord? They were praising the Lord because of His victory, even though they hadn't won the victory yet. John Calvin wrote, "Here the people are praised for obedience, and the faithfulness of God is, at the same time, celebrated. They testified their fidelity by shouting, because they were persuaded, that what God had commanded would not be in vain...."[54] That's why it is a shout of faith. They knew God had already given them the victory, so they claimed it!

Take No Loot

The Lord told Joshua that they were to take nothing from the city, that it was all accursed (Joshua 6:17–19). Normally, soldiers would take the spoils of a battle, but God said, "Not this city," because the whole city was given to the Lord.

And they burnt the city with fire, and all that was therein: only the silver, and the gold, and the vessels of brass and of iron, they put into the treasury of the house of the LORD.
—Joshua 6:24

Strongholds in Life

You may be thinking, *"What does this have to do with me?"* This chapter is about victory over a stronghold that blocked the progress of Israel into the promised land. Although they are unlikely to be made of stone, we all have spiritual strongholds in our lives, walls that need to come down. A stronghold is something, someone, or some circumstance in your life that's hindering you from having victory and keeping you from moving forward to your full inheritance in the Lord Jesus Christ. It's a giant fortress that God must tear down and remove from your life.

The Christian life involves challenge and conflict, whether we like it or not. Our enemy wages war against us constantly. The world, the flesh, and the devil (Ephesians 2:1–3) are united against Christ and His people, just as the nations in Canaan were united against Joshua and the nation of Israel. The book of Joshua is an excellent example of how to tear down the strongholds that are before you.

It Is a Spiritual Battle

The Apostle Paul spoke about strongholds in 2 Corinthians 10:3–4:

> *For though we walk in the flesh, we do not war after the flesh: (For the weapons of our warfare are not carnal, but mighty through God to the pulling down of strong holds;)....*

Paul spoke on a spiritual level, on a spiritual plane. A stronghold is not fazed by white knuckles or New Year's resolutions. The walls are thick.

Consider It with Christ

It was 1944, in the middle of World War II.[55] Sub-Lieutenant Hiroo Onoda of the Imperial Japanese army was ordered to stay on Lubang Island in the Philippines and hold it for the glory of the Emperor. So he did. The following year, the Allies bombed Hiroshima and Nagasaki, and the Japanese surrendered. Shortly after, the war ended, but unfortunately, he didn't know. He kept on fighting the next year and the next year. He was still fighting twenty-nine years after the end of World War II. He was totally unaware that the war had finished long ago. Even when the police searched through the jungle and used megaphones to ask him to surrender and stop shooting the locals, he refused to give up. It wasn't until 1974 when they brought in his wartime commanding officer to order him to surrender that he finally stopped fighting.

Do you know that it's over for Satan? Calvary was the devil's Hiroshima and Nagasaki. There at the cross, his kingdom was completely destroyed, but he hasn't stopped fighting. The most effective way to deal with Satan is to bring the wartime Commanding Officer Jesus to order him to surrender. That's why we need our Commanding Officer to help us deal with the strongholds that sin and Satan strategically place in our lives.

The first principle is to consider your stronghold with Christ, just as Joshua did. Study your situation honestly. God had miraculously parted the Jordan for the Israelites, and Joshua hadn't received divine instruction on what to do next. They were just outside the city of Jericho, and Joshua had never fought that kind of battle. They had none of the equipment that was necessary, humanly speaking, to overcome a stronghold. The only weapons they had were slings, arrows, and spears—certainly no threat for the walls of Jericho.

Joshua knew they had to defeat the city. The Jordan was swelling again. There was no turning back. If they didn't defeat Jericho, they were done. Suddenly, Joshua was startled by someone who came into his sphere of vision.

...behold, there stood a man over against him with his sword drawn in his hand: and Joshua went unto him, and said unto him, Art thou for us, or for our adversaries? And

he said, Nay; but as captain of the host of the LORD am I
now come. And Joshua fell on his face to the earth, and did
worship....

—*Joshua 5:13–14*

This was a divine visitation, a pre-incarnate appearance of the Lord Jesus Christ. The Captain of the army, the Lord Jesus Himself, had come. Fear was unthinkable. The first thing you need to know when overcoming strongholds is that God doesn't leave you alone in the battle. He comes to fight for you, and He comes to your aid. The question is not if He is on your side, but rather, are you on His side?

Consider His Presence in the Battle

At first, Joshua didn't recognize who He was, so he said to Him, "Art thou for us, or for our adversaries?" (Joshua 5:13). The response was: "Nay; but as captain of the host of the LORD am I now come" (Joshua 5:14). If this were just an angel, the angel would have said, "Stand up. Don't worship me. I am just God's messenger." But this wasn't just an angel; this was "the Angel of the LORD," an Old Testament appearance of Jesus Christ. The drawn sword is a symbol of judgment that was about to come. The Israelites would be the instrument of judicial punishment that would fall on the people of Jericho.

The Lord's presence confirmed His promise to Joshua:

There shall not any man be able to stand before thee all
the days of thy life: as I was with Moses, so I will be with

thee: I will not fail thee, nor forsake thee.

—*Joshua 1:5*

Joshua was not alone in the battle! The Lord had promised to be with him.

The Lord was also reminding him, "Joshua, you're not first in command. You are second in command." All of us need to be reminded about that. Every father, every mother, every pastor, every Christian leader is not first in command. You are second in command. First in command is the Lord Jesus Christ (Joshua 5:14). If we forget this fact, we will fall.

No matter what stronghold you are dealing with in your life, you are not alone. The Captain, the Lord of hosts, is with you. Confess your total inadequacy: "Lord, I can't handle this stronghold. I can't deal with this. I don't have the weapons to pull down this stronghold." You must recognize that the weapons of your warfare do not belong to you. The Lord carries them to the battle. Acknowledge His presence and worship Him.

Consider His Promise for the Battle

Jericho was locked up tighter than a drum against the Israelites. The Lord said, "You see, Joshua, I have already given this city into your hand" (Joshua 6:2, paraphrased). "I have given" is the prophetic perfect tense, a future tense that describes an action as if it were already accomplished. Once again, all Joshua had to do was listen to God's Word and obey orders, and God would do the rest.

This is a principle in the Christian life that you must

remember. In the Lord Jesus Christ, you already have victory. Victory is your point of origin, not your destination. Despite all his swagger, Satan knows he can't win. There's no reason to allow a stronghold to continue in your life when you know Satan is already defeated. This would be a good time to review your memorials of past victories and move into battle.

Circle It with Prayer

In 1961, the Soviets constructed a wall right through the middle of Germany. It was known as the Berlin Wall. It was a massive structure of cement, barbed wire, and stone. It stayed there for twenty-eight years. In one of the more dramatic speeches in the history of the world, President Reagan, in 1987, turned to that wall and said, "Mr. Gorbachev, tear down this wall." Two years later, in 1989, the Berlin Wall came tumbling down.

What Joshua and Israel were really saying as they were circling the city was: "Lord, this stronghold is Yours, and we are giving it to You. Lord, please tear down this wall!" When you have a stronghold in your life that's troubling you, you must encircle it with prayer. Say, "Lord, I can't seem to handle this stronghold. I don't have any wisdom, strength, or strategy to tear this thing down. Lord, I'm giving it to You. Would You please tear down this wall?"

You may be a parent who has a wayward, rebellious teenager or child. You have done everything you know to do with this child, and nothing works. You say, "I don't know how to reach my child. I don't know how to tear down this wall." Circle your child with prayer and give him or her to the Lord.

There's only one person who can change someone's heart, and that is the Sovereign God of heaven! Your stronghold could be a weakness, a besetting sin, a stubborn person, a physical sickness, or a crushing circumstance, anything that's hindering you from having victory. Circle it with prayer, dedicate it to God, and say, "Lord God, please tear down this wall!"

Claim It by Faith

Jericho was a sinful city. Your stronghold may be a stubborn sin in your life that you can't seem to overcome. It may be another problem. Whatever you are facing, circle it with prayer. Then thank and praise God for the victory you know in your heart He will bring. God wants you to live in victory. He doesn't want any of His children to live in defeat. Satan has already been defeated. You only need to read the end of the Book.

The church at Corinth was a troubled assembly. A conflict had developed between the church and its founder, Paul. There was internal strife in the church, as the epistle makes clear. However, the larger problem seems to have been that some in the community were leading the church into a view of things that was contrary to Paul's. This resulted in the questioning of Paul's authority and his gospel (Galatians).

Paul made what he would later describe as a painful visit in an attempt to correct the matter and bring reconciliation (2 Corinthians 2:1–2). The visit wasn't a successful one from Paul's perspective. Someone in the

Corinthian church, possibly one of the false apostles, openly insulted him (2 Corinthians 2:5–8, 10; 7:12). Saddened by the Corinthians' lack of loyalty to defend him, seeking to spare them further reproof, and hoping that time would bring them to their senses, Paul returned to Ephesus.

From Ephesus, Paul wrote what is known as the "severe letter" and sent it with Titus to Corinth (2 Corinthians 7:5–16). Leaving Ephesus after a riot sparked by Demetrius (Acts 19:23–20:1), Paul went to Troas to meet Titus (2 Corinthians 2:12–13). But Paul was so anxious for news of how the Corinthians had responded to the "severe letter" that he couldn't minister there, even though the Lord had opened the door (2 Corinthians 2:12; 7:5).

Here is a rare look at Paul. He was down; he was defeated. He couldn't preach, even though a door was opened to him, so he left for Macedonia to look for Titus (2 Corinthians 2:13). The church at Corinth had become a stronghold against Paul. He had some serious relationship problems. People there were attacking him and criticizing him. False apostles were spreading lies about him. It was a stronghold that was defeating Paul, but Paul trusted the Lord to do what he was unable to do. He circled it with prayer.

Now I Paul myself beseech you by the meekness and gentleness of Christ, who in presence am base among you, but being absent am bold toward you: But I beseech you, that I may not be bold when I am present with that confidence, wherewith I think to be bold against some, which think of us as if we walked according to the flesh. For though we walk in the flesh, we do not war after the flesh: (For the

> *weapons of our warfare are not carnal, but mighty*
> *through God to the pulling down of strong holds;) Casting*
> *down imaginations, and every high thing that exalteth it-*
> *self against the knowledge of God, and bringing into*
> *captivity every thought to the obedience of Christ....*
> **—2 Corinthians 10:1–5**

The weapons we use in this spiritual war are not siege engines, battering rams, catapults, or moving towers. We don't use fleshly weapons. The weapons we use are God's Word, His promise, prayer, faith, and praise to God.

To Paul's immense relief and joy, Titus met him with the news that the majority of the Corinthians had repented of their rebellion against Paul (2 Corinthians 7:7). Paul wrote in 2 Corinthians 2:14, "Now thanks be unto God, which always causeth us to triumph in Christ, and maketh manifest the savour of his knowledge by us in every place." Paul was saying that God is the one who always causes us to triumph in Christ!

In rejoicing over the victory given to Him in Christ, Paul used the analogy of the ancient Roman triumph. After winning a major battle, the victorious army would march into the city of Rome, possibly through a triumphal arch. All over the city, they would burn incense. It was called the "sweet smell of victory." You could smell it everywhere. That's what Paul was referring to when he wrote: "...maketh manifest the savour of his knowledge by us in every place" (2 Corinthians 2:14). What God did for Joshua and Israel and for Paul He will do for the strongholds in your life!

WORKBOOK

Chapter Five Questions

Question: Do you typically ask God to bless *your* plans, or do you ask Him to show you *His* plans? When has God called you to do something that didn't make sense from a human viewpoint? How were your patience, self-control, and obedience tested?

_____

_____

_____

_____

_____

_____

_____

_____

_____

Question: What are some times when choosing to be silent may be a powerful spiritual discipline in a believer's life? Why is this such a difficult discipline for most people? What is the power of silence in a culture filled with noise?

_____

_____

_____

_____

_____

_____

_____

_____

_____

_____

Journal: What is a spiritual stronghold that you are facing? How is God showing you His presence and power to overcome that stronghold? Write out your prayer of submissive dependence on Him and write down the promises that He has given to you.

_____

_____

_____

_____

_____

_____

_____

_____

_____

_____

_____

_____

Action: Look at these other examples in Scripture of God's people praising Him in faith before seeing the actualization of their victory:

- David after the attack of the Amalekites in 1 Samuel 30
- King Jehoshaphat marching to battle in 2 Chronicles 20
- Paul and Silas in the Philippian jail in Acts 16.

How will you praise God today for the victory you already have in Him?

Chapter Five Notes

CHAPTER SIX

Turning Trouble into Triumph
Joshua 7:1–8:35

Big Idea: *Sin brings more trouble than we can ever imagine, and it must be dealt with mercilessly.*

But the children of Israel committed a trespass in the accursed thing: for Achan, the son of Carmi, the son of Zabdi, the son of Zerah, of the tribe of Judah, took of the accursed thing: and the anger of the LORD was kindled against the children of Israel.

—Joshua 7:1

Achan didn't obey the Lord, and he robbed the Lord. How on earth could he do this? Well, sin makes you stupid. He had lust in his heart and thought that no one, not even God, would find out or care if he took something. His actions inferred that living as an Israelite in God's favor meant you could bend the rules. Achan's attitude was treacherous. Achan stole, and Israel sinned by ignoring his trespass.

Chapter 7 of the book of Joshua is all about the trouble Joshua and Israel faced as a result. In fact, the keyword in this whole chapter is the word *trouble*.

> *And Joshua said, Why hast thou troubled us? the LORD shall trouble thee this day. And all Israel stoned him with stones, and burned them with fire, after they had stoned them with stones. And they raised over him a great heap of stones unto this day. So the LORD turned from the fierceness of his anger. Wherefore the name of that place was called, The valley of Achor, unto this day.*
> —*Joshua 7:25–26*

The word *Achor* means "trouble."[56]

The Underlying Cause of Their Trouble

This trouble didn't arise out of nowhere, of course. We can identify a root cause, or source, from which the trouble stemmed.

The Problem of Sin

The ultimate root of the trouble for Joshua and Israel was the problem of sin. The trouble Israel experienced came in the form of a man by the name of Achan, who acted out. Interestingly, the name *Achan* also means "trouble."[57]

God not only held Achan accountable, but also held all of Israel accountable. One Old Testament scholar, James

Smith, said, "God considered Israel an organic unity. A sin by one brought guilt upon all."[58]

Everyone Suffered

One sin can affect multitudes. You will see how much damage this one sin brought to the Israelites in this story. Satan cannot prevail against God's people, but sin within the church can bring defeat. It's folly to believe that your sin affects only you. If you live with unconfessed and unforsaken sin, the whole church can be overcome.

The Pitfall of Success

Pride goeth before destruction, and an haughty spirit before a fall.

—Proverbs 16:18

Chapter 6 of Joshua ends with a great victory. It was clear that God Himself was with them. But then chapter 7 opens on a note of defeat. The Israelites began to assume that God would bless all their efforts without any requirements on their part. The most vulnerable time in your Christian walk may be right after you experience a great victory.

You probably don't know the name Bill Gramatica. He was a successful field-goal kicker for the Arizona Cardinals, but he is probably most remembered for one incident. On December 15, 2001, the Cardinals were playing the Giants.[59] As the first half came to a close,

Gramatica was called upon to attempt a 42-yard field goal. He kicked the ball straight down the middle, between the goal posts, for a three-point field goal. He was so happy that he jumped up in the air in celebration. It was one of those self-congratulatory leaps of joy: *"I did it! I can't believe how good a kicker I am!"* But upon landing, he blew out the ACL in his knee. He didn't kick again for the rest of the season. He missed it! The victory was followed by an agonizing defeat.

When you are on the mountaintop, raising your hands in victory, you become a bigger target for Satan. It sounds illogical, but if you are not careful, you can sometimes be defeated by your victories. Your guard is down, and Satan knows this is a prime time to attack.

The Peril of Self-Reliance

Joshua, being a good general, sent out a team of men on a reconnaissance mission. He wanted them to go up and spy out Ai to see what it was like (Joshua 7:2). You can almost hear the self-sufficiency and pride in their actions. *"We can handle this one."* Listen to the words of the spies when they returned from Ai: "...make not all the people to labour thither; for they are but few" (Joshua 7:3). There were 40,000 at Jericho and only 3,000 at Ai.

The Israelites were preoccupied with troop strength instead of trusting the Lord. When you stop relying upon the Lord, you start relying upon yourself. In this passage, we don't see that Joshua prayed. We don't see that they waited to get orders from the Lord. Their attitude changed. When you are not praying or seeking God, that's a sign of self-reliance.

If Joshua had led his men in a prayer meeting, he would have realized there was sin in the camp before they went into battle. God would have revealed that to him. But the Israelites didn't pray. In their self-reliance and pride, they took their eyes off the Lord, and they fell prey to judgment.

The Unexpected Curse

So there went up thither of the people about three thousand men: and they fled before the men of Ai.
—Joshua 7:4

Joshua and Israel marched into battle, and they fully expected to be victorious. They were not. When you are disobedient to the Lord, you are never prepared for battle! You will not have God's help and strength. When you are not walking in obedience, you are not going to have God's blessing.

Defeat

First of all, there will be defeat. They were not obeying God, so they suffered defeat. Sin and self-reliance always bring defeat. The battle is summarized in Joshua 7:4: "So there went up thither of the people about three thousand men: and they fled before the men of Ai." Ai was in the hill country, about fifteen miles from Jericho, and one went up to Ai because it was situated 1,700 feet above sea level. It's a steep march up rugged terrain. Trust me in this. I did some archaeology at this location, which is now called Khirbet el-Maqatir. Each day, we hiked up for about a mile to reach the site, and I thought of this passage. The Israelites marched confidently up the hill, but they soon came running back down in defeat, running for their lives. They marched up to Ai, beaming with confidence, and came down in humiliating defeat.

Death

> Then when lust hath conceived, it bringeth forth sin: and sin, when it is finished, bringeth forth death.
> —*James 1:15*

Sin and self-reliance bring not only defeat, but death. As Israel's army was retreating down this steep hill, the men of Ai had no mercy. Thirty-six men died on those mountain slopes. This is what happens when you leave the ark of the covenant home and go into battle without it. In Jericho, they followed God's orders. Here at Ai, they followed their own plan. At Jericho, they depended on God's strength. At Ai, they depended on their own military strength. Jericho was afraid of Israel. Israel was afraid of Ai. At Jericho, there were no deaths. Here, thirty-six men died.

Don't believe that your sin doesn't affect anyone else. Because of one man's sin, there were thirty-six widows in Israel, thirty-six families grieving over the loss of someone they loved. A law in God's economy is that death always follows sin. It may be someone else's death, but death follows sin as surely as night follows day.

Dismay, Despondency, and Doubt

Because of Achan's sin, Israel became like the Canaanites. They were afraid and alone without God to protect them. Sin causes you to live in perpetual fear. Man didn't experience fear until after sin in the Garden of Eden. Holiness produces boldness, but sin produces fear.

And Joshua rent his clothes, and fell to the earth upon his face before the ark of the LORD until the eventide, he and the elders of Israel, and put dust upon their heads. And Joshua said, Alas, O LORD God, wherefore hast thou at all brought this people over Jordan, to deliver us into the hand of the Amorites, to destroy us? would to God we had been content, and dwelt on the other side Jordan! O LORD, what shall I say, when Israel turneth their backs before their enemies! For the Canaanites and all the inhabitants of the land shall hear of it, and shall environ us round, and cut off our name from the earth: and what wilt thou do unto thy great name?

—Joshua 7:6-9

This was the first real defeat General Joshua had ever suffered. He was humble, prostrate before the Lord, and despondent. Had Joshua humbled himself *before* the battle, the situation would have been different *after* the battle.[60]

Up until this time, Joshua had never questioned God. He had always been the one who was strong in faith. This is another consequence of sin: it robs you of faith. You will start to doubt God and question Him. Do you remember when the twelve spies came back from the promised land? Ten gave a bad report, but Joshua and Caleb gave a good report (Numbers 13:25–33). Joshua was strong in faith, but after the defeat, he began to express doubt. He sounded just like one of those unbelieving Israelites in Kadesh Barnea (Numbers 13–14). Sin will bring unbelief and doubts.

The Bible says in Proverbs 19:3, "The foolishness of a man twists his way, and his heart frets against the LORD" (NKJV). Human nature likes to shift the blame, and that's exactly what was going on here. People were trying to blame their sin on everybody but themselves. It's always somebody else's fault. Everybody's a victim.

Dishonor

Joshua really got to the heart of the matter when he said, "Lord, our defeat is going to dishonor Your name" (Joshua 7:9, paraphrased). Joshua understood the connection: "Lord, if we are defeated, Your name will not receive honor." As a Christian, you are inseparably linked to God's name. Be sure that you don't bear it in vain. If you call yourself a Christian and live like the devil, that's taking the Lord's name in vain.

Imagine that you had the opportunity to write a new constitution for the United States of America, a constitution that would include a bill of rights containing ten declarations that would be the foundational precepts for a new nation. What would your first declaration be? The first thing on your list would probably be the thing you think is most important.

God did give such a document as He constituted His people to become a nation. In Exodus 20, God listed ten declarations that were foundational to the nation. On the top half of that list, God said, "Thou shalt not take the name of the LORD thy God in vain" (Exodus 20:7). This is supremely important to God. It's God's first concern. Therefore, it should be ours as well.

Taking God's name in vain is reflected in our manner of life, in the things we do. If you take God's name upon yourself, then you must be sure to reflect the character of the One whose name you have taken. In Exodus 20, when God made a covenant with Israel, Israel took upon itself the name of God. They became God's people, "a peculiar people," a nation of priests (1 Peter 2:9). Their new mission was to show the character and glory of God to the rest of the world by how they lived their lives. They were to be lights in the dark world. They had taken God's name, and they were to bear it to the world. God warned them not to take His name in vain. In other words, "Live up to the name you have taken!"

This principle applies not just to Israel, but also to Christians today. As God's people, our first concern is to honor His name. When the disciples asked Jesus to teach them how to pray, He taught them a pattern for prayer that we now know as the Lord's Prayer. In that prayer, Jesus placed a great emphasis on honoring God's name. The first petition in the prayer is "Hallowed be thy name" (Matthew 6:9). *Hallowed* is from the Greek word *hagizo*, meaning "to set apart as holy" or "to treat as holy."[61] This word is an imperative verb. It is a command! God's name is to be honored. When we live in defeat because of disobedience and sin, we are not honoring God's name. In fact, we are dishonoring His name, and that is a serious issue with God.

The Cure for Trouble in Your Life

The Lord allowed Joshua and his leaders to stay on their faces until the evening sacrifice. God allows you to come to the end of yourself in desperation before He intervenes and speaks.

And the LORD said unto Joshua, Get thee up; wherefore liest thou thus upon thy face?

—Joshua 7:10

God was about to give Joshua some practical steps for removing the trouble from his life and returning to triumph.

Investigation

The first thing God did was rebuke Joshua. Sometimes you just need a good rebuke from Almighty God to get you back on your feet and moving again. A spiritual self-examination often reveals the cause of trouble in your life. After that, it's no longer the time to stay in prayer. First, Joshua was prematurely proactive when he should have been prayerful. Then he was prayerful when it was time to be proactive. God said that He would not be with them until they took action to find the accursed thing that was stolen (Joshua 7:12). There's a time to intercede and a time to investigate. When God's hand of blessing is not with you, it's time to investigate the problem.

Revelation

To find the one who caused the trouble, Joshua began casting lots.[6263] The practice of casting lots is mentioned seventy times in the Old Testament and seven times in the New Testament. Despite the many references to this practice, it's not completely clear how it was done. Scholars disagree as to what might have been used. Some think sticks of various lengths could have been used. Others think it was flat stones or even coins that were cast. Some think that in Israel's case, the lots were two stones kept in a pocket behind the priest's breastplate. They were taken and cast down to the ground, just like a person would use dice today. The manner in which the stones landed would reveal God's will.

The two stones were called Urim and Thummin, meaning "Light" and "Perfection." Through them, the priest determined the mind of God. Regardless of what the lots were, Scripture affirms that they were used to determine God's will: "The lot is cast into the lap; but the whole disposing thereof is of the LORD" (Proverbs 16:33). We don't use them today because if we want to know the mind of God, we have a more sure word of prophesy. The Word of God and the Spirit of God reveal God's will to us today.

Tribe by tribe. Family by family. House by house. Man by man. Joshua whittled it down until finally the lot fell upon Achan. Why did they go through such a tedious process? Why didn't God just reveal his name and say, "Joshua, it's Achan." I think one reason was that God wanted to show Israel the seriousness of sin. The whole process brought fear into the hearts of the people, and God wanted to give a message. It's a serious thing to sin against Almighty God.

I think another reason is that it gave Achan an opportunity to come forward and confess. Instead, Achan waited out this whole process without saying a word. Why did he let it go on rather than confess? I think he had actually convinced himself that he was going to get away with it. Again, "...when lust hath conceived, it bringeth forth sin" (James 1:15). Then, like Adam hiding behind the fig leaves (Genesis 3:7–8) and David hiding behind his marriage to Bathsheba (2 Samuel 11–12), Achan tried to hide his sin. Incredible.

Many times, God will be patient and wait for you to come forward. But if you cover your sin, He will uncover it. That's exactly what He did with Achan.

> He that covereth his sins shall not prosper: but whoso confesseth and forsaketh them shall have mercy.
> **—Proverbs 28:13**

Achan probably rationalized that it wasn't wrong to take something from Jericho. Perhaps he thought, *"I'm a soldier. I deserve this. I deserve the spoils of war."* We need to remember Proverbs 21:2, which says, "Every way of a man is right in his own eyes: but the LORD pondereth the hearts."

First John 1:8 says, "If we say that we have no sin, we deceive ourselves, and the truth is not in us." Your mind works in overdrive to try to convince you that you are innocent. That's how you end up rationalizing.

You may believe that you have buried your sin and no one knows, but God knows. He will reveal your sin if you don't confess. Sometimes you forget that God sees all. Achan forgot that God sees all. *God sees all.*

Extermination

Achan and his whole family suffered tremendous judgment. Now, someone's going to say, "Wait a minute. In Joshua 7, verses 20 and 21, he confessed." Yes, but he confessed after the fact. He only confessed when he had no other choice.

Achan's death is a symbol of how the sin in your life must be exterminated. God doesn't want you to stay in the valley of trouble! If you want victory in your life, you must expose and express that sin. You must expel that sin and exterminate it. *Exterminate* means to destroy completely, as if down to the roots. There must be no trace left.

Rededication

In Joshua 8, the Israelites went back to Ai rather than bypassing it. This time, they were wiser. They prayed, they received their orders from God, and God gave them a battle plan. God's plan was to use a misdirection strategy. Israel attacked from the front and pretended they were defeated again, but a contingent of the Israelite army was hidden behind the city. Every man in the city pursued Israel, leaving Ai unprotected. The army in hiding entered Ai and burned the city. When the men of Ai turned and saw their city ablaze, it absolutely demoralized them. The fleeing Israelite army turned back on the men of Ai, who were then caught in the middle and attacked on each side. No Ai soldier escaped. The spoils were taken from the city, and the king was executed and publicly displayed (Joshua 8:14–29). Where there had been defeat, now there was victory! Joshua and the people of Israel rededicated themselves to the Lord (Joshua 8:30–35).

After the victory at Ai, Joshua led Israel to a valley thirty miles north of Ai, up through the Jordan valley. On one side was Mount Ebal, and on the other side was Mount Gerizim. Why this place? The valley at the base of these two mountains formed a perfect natural amphitheater. The limestone strata were broken into a succession of ledges so as to present the appearance of a series of benches. James Montgomery Boice wrote, "One feature of the place between the mountains is its fine acoustical properties. A person on one mountain can easily hear a person on the other, and both can clearly hear what goes on below."[64]

Joshua divided the twelve tribes of Israel and put six tribes on one mountain and six on the other. On Mount Gerizim were the tribes of Simeon, Levi, Judah, Issachar, Joseph, and Benjamin. On Mount Ebal were the tribes of Reuben, Gad, Asher, Zebulun, Dan, and Naphtali. The ark of the covenant was set in the valley, and the leaders of Israel were there. They were all facing the ark, a symbol of God's presence. Then Joshua read from Deuteronomy. He read the law of God.

As Joshua read the blessings, all the people on Mount Gerizim said, "Amen!" As Joshua read the curses, all the people on Mount Ebal said, "Amen." This was a giant object lesson for every person in Israel. Obedience to God's law brings blessings, but disobedience brings curses.

Joshua and Israel renewed their dedication to obeying God. However, the curse of sin had to be removed. On Mount Ebal, an altar had been built (Deuteronomy 27:4; Joshua 8:30–32). It was made of huge stones and covered in plaster. The law of God was written on it. This, too, would serve as a giant object lesson. In order for the curse of sin to be removed, something innocent had to bear the curse, be sacrificed, and die for that sin. This pointed to the future, to the cross, when the innocent Son of God would bear the curse of sin, redeem mankind from the curse, and replace it with blessing.

I remember witnessing to a man years ago. I couldn't get him to understand his need for Christ. Every time I started to tell him about Jesus Christ, he would say, "God doesn't like me. God is against me. God hates me." He said, "Preacher, I am cursed." I tried to tell him that God loves him and wants to save him, but it never registered.

One day when I was driving him to church, I was again trying to share the gospel, and he again started to say, "God has cursed me. I am cursed." He looked at me, waiting for me to disagree with him as I normally did.

But this time, I looked at him and said, "You are right.

You are cursed!"

He was shocked that I agreed. He said, "You mean you agree with me?"

"Yes, I absolutely agree. You are cursed!"

"I knew it! I am cursed. Preacher, why? Why am I cursed?"

I read to him Galatians 3:10.

He said, "Oh no, now what? What am I going to do?"

"You have to get the curse removed."

"How do I do that?"

"Well, you can't remove the curse, but I know someone who can."

"Who? Do you think he will remove it for me?"

Then I read him Galatians 3:13. I said, "The only way for the curse to be removed is through Jesus Christ."

Finally, it dawned on him why Jesus Christ was so important and why he needed Him! Christ is able to remove from our lives the curse of sin and the trouble it brings and replace it with a mountain of blessings. Has Christ removed the curse for you?

Chapter 7 of Joshua opens with a valley of trouble, but in chapter 8, the story closes on a mountain of triumph! This story should be an encouragement to us all because, let's face it, we all fail. We all bring trouble on ourselves because of our foolish mistakes, but failure is not final in the Christian life. Joshua and Israel didn't stay in the valley of trouble. They turned their trouble into triumph by dealing thoroughly with sin in the camp.

Have you ever failed in your Christian walk? Have you ever suffered defeat? We serve such a wonderful God that He is able to turn all our defeats into victories. When you are defeated, God wants you to get up and begin again, more wisely this time.

The perfect time to renew your heart's desire to obey the Lord is right after you have had a defeat. If you are in the valley of trouble, get out of it and go to the mountains of triumph! Let it be a door of hope. Confess your sin and self-reliance and dedicate yourself to a renewed obedience of God. Say, "I will obey the Lord."

You can have victory. God will forgive and restore you because Jesus' sacrifice paid your sin debt. Jesus Himself bore all your defeats and failures on the cross, so walk in the victory the Lord Jesus offers you!

WORKBOOK

Chapter Six Questions

Question: Who suffered because of Achan's sin? Describe a time when one person's sin caused trouble for an entire family, church, organization, or even nation. Have you ever committed a sin that you thought would only affect you but ended up hurting others?

_____

_____

_____

_____

_____

_____

_____

_____

Question: What are the victories in your life? What are the things that you feel confident you can handle? Have these become points of vulnerability because you are depending on yourself instead of the Lord?

_____

_____

_____

_____

_____

_____

_____

_____

_____

Journal: Write out a prayer of dependence on and rededication to the Lord. Ask Him for wisdom concerning those areas of your life that you think you already have all figured out. Are you struggling with any doubts or unbelief? Ask God to reveal to you any underlying sin that has damaged your faith. Ask Him to guide you in investigating areas where you are experiencing trouble and to reveal to you any hidden sin.

_____

_____

_____

_____

_____

_____

_____

_____

_____

_____

Action: Do a study through Scripture of what God has to say about His name and reputation. Where else is an appeal to the honor of God's name used in prayer? How well are you wearing and bearing the name of Christ?

Chapter Six Notes

_____

_____

_____

_____

_____

_____

_____

_____

_____

_____

_____

_____

_____

_____

_____

_____

_____

_____

_____

_____

CHAPTER SEVEN

The Devil's Moldy Bread
Joshua 9:1–27

Big Idea: *You are vulnerable to deception if you are not committed to daily prayer and study of God's Word.*

I can remember being taught in junior high science class to be very cautious with chemicals. Not every chemical is what it appears to be. For example, one chemical that looks exactly like water is hydrochloric acid. The chemical makeup of water is H_2O. The chemical makeup of hydrochloric acid is H_2SO_4. Our teacher taught us a little poem about this important distinction that was designed to warn us to be careful when discerning chemicals:

Shed a tear for Jimmy Brown
Poor Jimmy is no more

For what he thought was H_2O
Was H_2SO_4.

Looks can be deceiving! There's an old saying: "All that glitters is not gold."

This is a story about deception. One of the ways I know the Bible is God's Word is that it's so very candid about the people who are in it, including its heroes. The Bible records, without bias, not only victories, but also the faults and failures of heroes. The Bible does that to help you deal with your own failures. Sometimes I make a mistake or fail, and I need to know there are other people who traveled that same road before me. They messed up, yet the Lord helped them through their failures. That's what we see with Joshua.

The Deception of the Enemy

One of the themes throughout the book of Joshua is that the Lord fights your battles, yet here is another instance of Joshua and Israel leaning on their own understanding instead of trusting in the Lord. They allowed themselves to be deceived when it could easily have been avoided. The way the Gibeonites deceived Joshua is also the way Satan still deceives the people of God, the way he deceives you and me.

And it came to pass, when all the kings which were on this side Jordan, in the hills, and in the valleys, and in all the coasts of the great sea over against Lebanon, the Hittite, and the Amorite, the Canaanite, the Perizzite, the Hivite,

and the Jebusite, heard thereof; That they gathered them-
selves together, to fight with Joshua and with Israel, with
one accord.

—Joshua 9:1–2

All the kings of the Canaanites came together in one big confederacy to defend themselves. Verse 2 says that they came together "with one accord." When the Canaanites heard about Jericho and Ai, they put aside their petty differences and came together to fight against Joshua. The church can learn a lesson from these Canaanites. However, when the Gibeonites considered warfare with Israel, they sensed it was better to avoid it, so they created an opportunity. They knew this was a perfect time to pull off a deception.

As a Hivite city, Gibeon was on Joshua's list to be destroyed, according to Deuteronomy 20. In the law, there's a stipulation that Joshua and Israel could make peace with peoples and cities outside the border of the promised land. Somehow the Gibeonites knew about this law, and they were going to use it to their own advantage.

Likewise, the enemy knows the Word of God and can twist it to use it against you. We see Satan quoting Scripture when he came to tempt the Lord Jesus Christ after He fasted for forty days in the wilderness (Matthew 4:1–11). Satan knows exactly when and where to strike.

The Gibeonites also knew that Joshua and Israel would be focused on the Canaanite confederacy. Joshua and the elders of Israel would probably welcome an alliance with a people that could help them. We are most vulnerable to deception when we are being bombarded with a big problem or are stressed out because of a big obstacle. Just as the Gibeonites knew Joshua was vulnerable, Satan also knows. When our energy and focus are diverted to something, the enemy subtly moves in. Part of Satan's deception is his timing.

Deceitful Look

And when the inhabitants of Gibeon heard what Joshua had done unto Jericho and to Ai, They did work wilily, and went and made as if they had been ambassadors, and took old sacks upon their asses, and wine bottles, old, and rent, and bound up; And old shoes and clouted upon their feet, and old garments upon them; and all the bread of their provision was dry and mouldy.

—Joshua 9:3–5

The Gibeonites pretended to be an official delegation from a foreign land to make peace with Joshua. They wore old, ragged clothes. They brought dry, moldy bread. They used donkeys instead of horses because donkeys were better for a long journey. They had wineskins that were ripped and sewn together. Wine was put into certain animal skins. As the wine began to ferment over a long period of time, the skins would expand. Sometimes they would rip. They would then have to be discarded or sewn. The Gibeonites did all of this to look as if they had been traveling a long, long way to Joshua.

F. B. Meyer wrote, "It is in this way that we are tempted still—more by the wiles of Satan than by his open assaults; more by the deceitfulness of sin than by its declared war. And it is little matter for wonder that those who succeed at Jericho and Ai fall into the nets woven and laid down by the wiles of Gibeon."[65] Satan is a master of masquerade. He knows exactly the right appearance designed to take you in. Paul warned us in the New Testament to beware:

> *And no marvel; for Satan himself is transformed into an angel of light. Therefore it is no great thing if his ministers also be transformed as the ministers of righteousness; whose end shall be according to their works.*
> —*2 Corinthians 11:14–15*

Deceitful Lies

> *And they said unto him, From a very far country thy servants are come because of the name of the LORD thy God: for we have heard the fame of him, and all that he did in Egypt....*
> —*Joshua 9:9*

Satan is "the father of lies," and he teaches his children to lie (John 8:44 ESV). If you try to deceive others, you become like him. In this story, the Gibeonites told several lies.

They were not from a far country. They were neighbors.

They told Joshua that they were his servants, rather than his enemies. Satan wants you to believe that he is your friend and your servant. He is not. He is your enemy.

In Genesis 3, Satan gave Eve the impression that he was trying to help her.

They were not there because of the name of God. They were not there to worship God. They were there to save their own skins. They knew exactly what Joshua wanted to hear, so that's what they told him. Lying seems to have become a way of life for them!

> *...for we have heard the fame of him, and all that he did in Egypt, And all that he did to the two kings of the Amorites, that were beyond Jordan, to Sihon king of Heshbon, and to Og king of Bashan, which was at Ashtaroth.*
> —*Joshua 9:9–10*

You may say, "Where is the lie there?" The lie is not in what they said; it's in what they *didn't* say. Notice that they said nothing about Jericho and Ai when they were reporting to Joshua. They left out those parts because they knew that if they mentioned them, Joshua would have been able to tell that they weren't from a far-off country.

One of the ways Satan loves to lie is to give you half of the truth, but not all of the truth. He will be silent about the other half. You can lie with words or without words. Truth is not only violated by falsehood; it can be equally outraged by silence.

Deceitful Logic

> *This our bread we took hot for our provision out of our houses on the day we came forth to go unto you; but now,*

behold, it is dry, and it is mouldy....

—Joshua 9:12

They were saying, "Look for yourself, Joshua. Judge for yourself. Elders, look at our clothes. Look how tattered they are. Look at this moldy bread. Look at our wineskins. Use your own eyes to make a logical conclusion." Satan wants you to rely on your own reason. He will feed you false information, and then he will say, "Now you make the judgment. Use your own logic, your own reason. You can figure out for yourself what to do." People don't have to sell out to Satan. If you are not doing things God's way and seeking Him for truth, you are opening yourself up to deception. This doesn't mean you shouldn't use your own reason, common sense, and logic. God gave you a brain to think, and you should use it, but you must also look to God. You need to pray. You must depend on God to show you His leading and on the power of the Holy Spirit.

Trust in the LORD with all thine heart; and lean not unto thine own understanding. In all thy ways acknowledge him, and he shall direct thy paths.
—Proverbs 3:5–6

The Decision of the Elders

And the men took of their victuals, and asked not counsel at the mouth of the LORD. And Joshua made peace with

them, and made a league with them, to let them live: and
the princes of the congregation sware unto them.
—*Joshua 9:14–15*

Joshua and the elders seemed to consider the proposal of the Gibeonites, but they made a foolish decision. The essence of leadership is making right decisions. The decisions we make as leaders don't just affect us; they affect multitudes. Therefore, decisions must be made cautiously and with wisdom. Seeking God's wisdom in decision-making cannot be overemphasized.

Wisdom as taught in Scripture focuses on the practical. It's not something theoretical and abstract. It's something that exists only when a person thinks and acts according to the truth as he or she makes the many choices that life demands. Life is made up of decisions, some major and some minor, and in a very real sense, the sum of our lives is the result of the decisions we make. This is especially true if one is a leader.

The ancients knew this. That's why wisdom literature was written to teach people how to make the right decisions in life. Scripture makes it clear that "the fear of the LORD is the beginning of wisdom" (Proverbs 9:10). Good, godly choices begin with a proper reverence and acknowledgement of God. If we are not careful, we can forget this and make foolish decisions because we don't begin with the fear of the Lord. Incredibly, this is what happened to Joshua and the elders. There are several reasons why their decision regarding the Gibeonites was a foolish one.

Prompt Decision

We don't read here of a time of waiting. Joshua and the elders made the decision quickly. Admittedly, there are certain decisions that have to be made in the spur of the moment when very little or no time is available to deliberate, but most major decisions are not that immediate. There was no reason for Joshua to make an immediate decision here.

Be careful about making a quick decision, especially if it has great ramifications. Don't be forced into a quick decision. If it's God's will today, it will be God's will tomorrow, and it will be God's will next week. True faith involves exercising patience. There have been times when others have attempted to force me into a quick decision that would have major ramifications. In cases like that, my answer is always "no." If I don't have time to pray over it and consult with God in prayer, then I don't believe it is of God. I heard the great preacher Adrian Rogers say on several occasions, "God never shouts, and He never shoves." God never shoves us into making major decisions quickly.

Presumptuous Decision

It was a presumptuous decision. Joshua 9:14 says that "the men took of their victuals," meaning they ate the moldy bread the Gibeonites offered to them. Scholars suggest two reasons why they ate this bread. Some believe this was a covenant meal. Whenever Israel made a covenant treaty agreement with a foreign power, they always shared a meal. These scholars believe that's why the Gibeonites brought the bread and the wine. They were expecting to have a meal together. Others believe the Israelites were inspecting the bread to find out if it was indeed moldy so they could validate the Gibeonites' claims.[66] Either way you look at it, the bottom line is that they ate the bread and swallowed the ruse—hook, line, and sinker.

Donald Campbell wrote, "Joshua and the Israelite leaders made at least two major mistakes. First, they trusted evidence that was highly questionable. Envoys with power to conclude treaties with other nations should have substantial credentials. It was foolish for Joshua not to demand such credentials."[67]

The Bible says in Proverbs that "the simple believeth every word" (Proverbs 14:15). If this group of men had been an authentic official delegation, it would have comprised a much larger company bearing adequate supplies, including sufficient provisions for the trip home. Real ambassadors would have thrown away their dry, moldy bread because their servants would have baked fresh bread for them. As officials, they would have packed the proper attire so they could make the best possible impression as they negotiated with the enemy. You will notice that Joshua and the elders only asked two questions and simple ones at that:

And the men of Israel said unto the Hivites, Peradventure ye dwell among us; and how shall we make a league with you? And they said unto Joshua, We are thy servants. And

Joshua said unto them, Who are ye? and from whence come ye?

—*Joshua 9:7-8*

With those questions, they were satisfied! The elders made a major decision on very little information, and it was a decision that would affect the lives of multitudes for centuries.

Prayerless Decision

*And the men took of their victuals, and **asked not counsel at the mouth of the LORD.***

—*Joshua 9:14* (emphasis added)

Now for the biggest mistake. The only time the Israelites got themselves into trouble was when they didn't seek God. They had fallen into the peril of prayerlessness before when they decided to go after Ai without asking God, and they were making the same mistake again.

It would have been easy to seek God. It wasn't a long, complicated process. Do you remember how the high priest had a little pocket in his breastplate with two stones in it (Exodus 28:30)? All Joshua and the elders had to do was have the high priest take those stones, cast the lots, and ask, "Lord, should we make an agreement with these men?" It was that simple, but they didn't do it. They didn't pray about it, and they suffered for it.

Pray about everything, even seemingly no-brainer decisions. Pray about every decision you make. Prayer should be your priority.

*...but in every thing by prayer and supplication with
thanksgiving let your requests be made known unto God.*
—*Philippians 4:6*

Permanent Decision

*We have sworn unto them by the LORD God of Israel: now
therefore we may not touch them.*
—*Joshua 9:19*

Notice that there were no conditions put on this treaty.
It was a solemn oath that could not be broken. The decision was permanent.

The Discovery of the Error

*And it came to pass at the end of three days after they had
made a league with them, that they heard that they were
their neighbours, and that they dwelt among them. And
the children of Israel journeyed, and came unto their cities
on the third day. Now their cities were Gibeon, and
Chephirah, and Beeroth, and Kirjathjearim.*
—*Joshua 9:16–17*

Can you imagine? After three days, the Israelites
started to get reports: "Remember those guys who came
from a far country? Guess what. It's not as far as we
thought it was." They began to check it out. As they continued their journey, they came to these Gibeonite cities,
and they said, "Oh no, what have we done?"

Immediate Contention and Loss

This brought contention immediately. The people were murmuring because they were angry at the princes for the covenant they had made. Bad decisions cause murmuring. It cost them financially. Because of this covenant they made, plunder normally taken by soldiers from these defeated cities as a means of their own sustenance and wealth was gone. It also had the potential to cost them spiritually. Being their neighbors, these Canaanites, who worshiped idols, could be a thorn in their flesh and lead them away from the Lord.

You do have to give these leaders credit for at least being men of their word. They knew God takes oaths seriously. To violate that oath would have been to take the holy name of God in vain, and this would have brought divine judgment.

The Eventual Curse

If we fast-forward four hundred years through the history of Israel, we see that Saul had killed some of the Gibeonites during his reign (2 Samuel 21:1–9). Then, because Saul had broken the oath of Joshua, Israel experienced a famine for three years under King David. The Gibeonites demanded that David hand over some of Saul's male descendants to be executed. It cost seven lives for the curse to be made right and the famine to end.

This biblical event illustrates how the consequences of some bad decisions seem to linger on for generations. That's a sobering thought, and it should give us pause. I don't want my bad decisions to affect people adversely long after I'm gone. In fact, I would much prefer the opposite. Good decisions, godly decisions, can also have an impact for generations to come.

This leads to the next point. Joshua took a bad situation and made a good decision in it. Great leaders are those who make good second decisions. We won't always get first decisions right, but we can make a good second decision. With God's help, all things can work together for good.

Comfort Brought Providentially

For Joshua and the Israelites, the episode didn't end on a negative note. Our God can take all the bad things in life and turn them to good!

Joshua said to the Gibeonites, "Wherefore have ye beguiled us, saying, We are very far from you; when ye dwell among us? Now therefore ye are cursed, and there shall none of you be freed from being bondmen, and hewers of wood and drawers of water for the house of my God" (Joshua 9:22–23). What a statement! They were going to be servants. Think about it. When you are making sacrifices to the Lord in the house of the Lord, there are two things you constantly need: wood for burning and water for cleansing. Somebody had to cut down the trees and hew the wood. Somebody had to draw and bring the water.

As a result of these tasks that placed them close to the house of the Lord, the Gibeonites learned to worship God. They put away their idols. This meant they were no longer an idolatrous threat to sway the people of Israel. In fact, if you trace the history of Israel, you will find that the Gibeonites were at times more faithful than the Israelites. Later they were called the Nethinim, meaning "the given ones," because they were assistants to the priests. They were committed to the house of God.

When the Lord divided up the land, He gave Gibeon to the Levites and Aaron. Four hundred years later, David put the tabernacle in the city of Gibeon. It was at the altar in Gibeon that God appeared to Solomon and granted his request for wisdom. In the days of Nehemiah, the Gibeonites were mentioned as among the people who helped to rebuild the walls of Jerusalem. According to Ezra 2:43 and 8:20, the Gibeonites were so faithful in their service to the temple that they replaced the Levites for a time.

God can turn curses into blessings. God can take your bad and foolish decisions and bring good out of them.

> *And we know that all things work together for good to them that love God, to them who are the called according to his purpose.*
> **—Romans 8:28**

A friend once told me a story about a mistake he made while driving home one night. He took a wrong turn and got lost. He decided just to continue driving and see where that road took him. Eventually, the road he was on intersected with the road he wanted.

God spoke to him then, saying, "If you trust Me, I will put you back on the right road as if you had never made a wrong decision in the first place. If you just trust Me, I will put you on the right road." Our God is like that. When you make a mistake, He will put you back on the right road if you trust Him.

Lessons to Learn

1. Always take your time making big decisions. Proverbs 12:8 says, "A man shall be commended according to his wisdom: but he that is of a perverse heart shall be despised."

2. Don't depend solely upon the counsel of man. It's normally a good idea to have several people's advice, but here in the book of Joshua, it was a case in which all of the wise elders of Israel were wrong! God's Word and His leading take precedence over man's input.

3. Always keep your word, even if it costs you.

4. Don't depend upon your own reasoning alone. Use common sense, but ultimately look to the Lord.

5. Always, always, always pray for direction. Remember Proverbs 3:5–6 and trust in God to guide you.

6. If you have already made a bad decision, repent, ask forgiveness, and commit it to God. He can turn curses into blessings!

God is a good Father, and He has your best interest in mind. He wants to lead and guide you on the best path. You can trust Him. He won't lead you astray. Set your heart to depend on God to guide you through this life. Don't make decisions without consulting Him. Allow Him to redirect you if you make mistakes. You won't regret trusting Him with the direction of your life!

WORKBOOK

Chapter Seven Questions

Question: Describe a time when you were deceived. How did you feel when you realized the truth? How was your life permanently affected by decisions you made while you were deceived? What did you learn through that experience?

_____

_____

_____

_____

_____

_____

_____

_____

Question: Psalm 15:4 talks about a person who "sweareth to his own hurt, and changeth not." When you give your word, can others count on you to follow through, even if new information becomes available or your situation changes? Why is being a man or woman of your word so important to God?

_____

_____

_____

_____

_____

_____

_____

_____

_____

Journal: What are some guidelines from the Bible about how to make wise decisions? Write out a process to use when you are faced with a major choice.

_____

_____

_____

_____

_____

Action: What does the Bible say about false prophets and deceivers? (Some passages to start your study include Matthew 7:15–20, Matthew 24:5, 2 Timothy 3:1–7, 2 Peter 2:1–3, and 1 John 4:1–4.) Learn about how cults and false teachers draw people into their deception and how believers can protect themselves with the truth. A great resource for this is *World Religions and Cults: Counterfeits of Christianity* by Bodie Hodge and Roger Patterson.

Chapter Seven Notes

CHAPTER EIGHT

The Longest Day
Joshua 10:1–43

Big Idea: *God is willing to move heaven and earth to fight on behalf of His people.*

Have you ever heard someone say, "It's been a long day"? What we mean by this is that it's been a tough day or we've had a difficult time. In the literal sense, there's no such thing as a long day. Every day is twenty-four hours. But there was a day in history that was truly a long day in the literal sense. It was the longest day, much longer than twenty-four hours. It's recorded in the Word of God in Joshua 10. It was a day when the sun stood still.

This is one of the greatest miracles of the Bible. Critics of the Bible who don't believe in miracles seek to explain it away. No story has been ridiculed or abused more than this story of Joshua's long day. Some argue that this story disproves the authenticity of the Bible, but in my opinion, it actually does the opposite. It upholds, accentuates, emphasizes, and exalts the authenticity of the Bible. Let's take a close look at the miracle of the long day.

As we read earlier, the Gibeonites made a peace treaty with Joshua. Gibeon had deceived Joshua and the elders, but the Israelites nevertheless made a binding agreement with them. Israel and Gibeon were now allies, not enemies. That meant Gibeon, a large and strong city, would fight on the side of Israel, not against it.

Five Amorite kings had heard of Israel's success in Jericho and Ai. They knew they would have a hard time prevailing in battle, especially with Gibeon becoming Israel's ally, so the kings of the Amorites formed a confederacy and together planned to eliminate Gibeon before Israel arrived (Joshua 10:1–4).

Therefore the five kings of the Amorites, the king of Jerusalem, the king of Hebron, the king of Jarmuth, the king of Lachish, the king of Eglon, gathered themselves together, and went up, they and all their hosts, and encamped before Gibeon, and made war against it.

—Joshua 10:5

The Gibeonites were suddenly threatened by an overwhelming force bearing down on them. You might say that they jumped from the frying pan into the fire! Now what? They sent a runner with a message to Joshua: Help!

The Miracle of the Long Day

You have to admire Joshua. He could have thought, *"Here's my chance to get out of that agreement that I made with these Gibeonites. I can just let them be slaughtered by these five kings, and that whole episode will be over.*" But Joshua didn't do that because he had given his word. Joshua was a man of integrity, so he decided to help Gibeon. He gathered his forces together. Joshua now had to face a confederacy of five kings. This was a formidable force of Amorite soldiers and warriors.

A Forceful Plan

Joshua undoubtedly got his plans from the Lord because he had learned about going into battle without first consulting God. The army wasted no time. Normally it was a three-day journey to Gibeon from Gilgal, but these soldiers made the march in just one night. Joshua 10:7 says that they "ascended." That's because geographically this was a march into the hill country, ascending about 4,000 feet. They ran all through the night to get there so quickly.

Doubtless when they finally arrived, they were exhausted. The plan was to attack the enemy coalition by surprise, but would they be able to put up a fight after an all-night march? It was at this moment that God gave them a promise:

And the LORD said unto Joshua, Fear them not: for I have delivered them into thine hand; there shall not a man of them stand before thee.
—Joshua 10:8

Sound familiar? Doesn't that sound like when God told Joshua in the beginning, "There shall not any man be able to stand before thee" (Joshua 1:5)? God later said, "I have given into thine hand Jericho, and the king thereof, and the mighty men of valour" (Joshua 6:2). In Joshua 10:8, God reaffirmed His promise. He had not changed His mind.

The Furious Pursuit

And the LORD discomfited them before Israel, and slew them with a great slaughter at Gibeon, and chased them along the way that goeth up to Bethhoron, and smote them to Azekah, and unto Makkedah. And it came to pass, as they fled from before Israel, and were in the going down to Bethhoron, that the LORD cast down great stones from heaven upon them unto Azekah, and they died: they were more which died with hailstones than they whom the children of Israel slew with the sword.

—Joshua 10:10–11

Joshua took the Amorites by surprise, and the Lord gave the Israelites victory. The southern confederacy of kings and soldiers soon realized they were defeated, and they ran from the battle. As they ran, the Lord pelted them with huge hailstones, and many were killed—more even than those killed in battle. To me, the miraculous thing about this is that God hit the enemy with hailstones, but not any of the Israelites. Have you ever been in a hailstorm in which you weren't getting hit when everyone else around you was?

Joshua realized he had an unprecedented opportunity

to smash the southern confederacy of kings and to open up the land of Canaan for all the children of Israel. Although the Amorite armies were defeated at Gibeon, the cities were full of people who also needed to be slain to fulfill God's command. However, Joshua was losing daylight. Some of these soldiers and kings could escape under the cover of darkness and regroup.

A Faith-Filled Prayer

Then spake Joshua to the LORD in the day when the LORD delivered up the Amorites before the children of Israel, and he said in the sight of Israel, Sun, stand thou still upon Gibeon; and thou, Moon, in the valley of Ajalon. And the sun stood still, and the moon stayed, until the people had avenged themselves upon their enemies. Is not this written in the book of Jasher? So the sun stood still in the midst of heaven, and hasted not to go down about a whole day.
—Joshua 10:12-13

James Montgomery Boice thoroughly described this point in the battle when he wrote:[68]

Picture the scene that must have greeted Joshua as he crested the ridge of Beth Horon. Before him, as far as his eyes could see, was masses of the panicked armies being pursued by his own soldiers. Over the slopes and above the plains beyond, there was a great cloud from which hail was falling. To his right, the sun was beginning its long afternoon decent towards the Mediterranean. Joshua must have realized two things. First, this was an unprecedented opportunity to destroy the southern confederacy. The best of their soldiers had come out against him, and they were fleeing. If he could destroy them now, the southlands would be open to his advancing armies.

At the same time, he must have recognized that the day was escaping. When the sun set, fighting would cease, and there was not enough time before sunset to achieve total victory.

Joshua remembered God's promise, and faith welled up in his soul. What amazes me is the bold prayer that Joshua made. He asked God to make the sun stand still. How many of us would have the boldness to ask God for something so incredible? But doesn't Scripture challenge us to do such things?

> *I am the LORD thy God, which brought thee out of the land of Egypt: open thy mouth wide, and I will fill it.*
> —*Psalm 81:10*

> *Call unto me, and I will answer thee, and show thee great and mighty things, which thou knowest not.*
> —*Jeremiah 33:3*

The day stretched on and the sun didn't go down until the Israelites had defeated their enemies. What an incredible miracle! What an incredible thing, the miracle of the long day, the constancy of God's presence and favor. Verse 14 says that there's never been a day like it, not before and not since.

The Mystery of the Long Day

Joshua's long day is a mystery that many cannot accept. There are numerous variations people use to explain it more to their liking. All the debate seems to center around one question: What really happened? The implication of the question is doubt.

Literal or Not?

Some argue that this story can't be taken literally because Joshua said to the sun, "Stand still." Everyone knows it's a scientific fact that the earth, not the sun, is revolving, which gives us daytime and nighttime. If one wants to get literal, it could be argued that the sun doesn't actually move. All of God's created universe moves. The sun moves at a tremendous rate of speed. So, was Joshua wrong to speak to the sun? The Hebrew reads, "Sun, stop acting. Sun, cease acting."[69] The sun's gravitational pull is what causes the earth to rotate, so in speaking to the sun, Joshua was scientifically correct. Some say that the fact that he addressed the sun in this way, as if commanding it, makes his prayer suspect. But events and language in Scripture can be scientifically correct, even if the people of the time had no way of knowing a scientific explanation.

The more plausible argument is that Joshua was simply using the language of observation. When a character in Scripture uses the language of observation, it doesn't mean the Bible is scientifically inaccurate. A document that every Christian should become acquainted with is the Chicago Statement on Biblical Inerrancy. It's a significant document that clarifies the doctrine of the inspiration and inerrancy of Scripture. Great men of God—scholars, preachers, and seminary professors—drafted this document. It comprises nineteen articles that summarize the inerrancy of Scripture. Article XIII reads thus:[70]

> We affirm the propriety of using inerrancy as a theological term with reference to the complete truthfulness of Scripture.
>
> We deny that it is proper to evaluate Scripture according to standards of truth and error that are alien to its usage or purpose. We further deny that inerrancy is negated by Biblical phenomena such as a lack of modern technical precision, irregularities of grammar or spelling, observational descriptions of nature, the reporting of falsehoods, the use of hyperbole and round numbers, the topical arrangement of material, variant selections of material in parallel accounts, or the use of free citations.

We must allow for the use of the language of observation in Scripture. People use the language of observation today when communicating with one another. Listen to your weatherman. He tells you the time of sunrise and sunset. Do you call the news station and say that he's scientifically inaccurate and, therefore, lying?

Laws of Nature

Critics say, "We can't take this event literally because this is against the laws of nature." Friend, there's no such thing as the laws of nature, only the laws of God. God doesn't operate according to the laws of nature. Nature operates according to the laws of God, and God can do whatever He wants! In the final analysis, you can't use the laws of nature to try to deny a miracle. Free yourself from thinking that way. You can't explain a miracle in earthly terms. Theologian Wayne Grudem argued that the laws of nature are synonymous with the term *providence*. Grudem defined providence as follows:[71]

God is continually involved with all created things in such a way that he (1) keeps them existing and maintaining the properties with which he created them; (2) cooperates with created things in every action, directing their distinctive properties to cause them to act as they do; and (3) directs them to fulfill his purposes.

Grudem proposed that a miracle is simply an extension of the providence of God. It's a less common kind of God's providential work that "arouses people's awe and wonder and bears witness to himself."[72] To speak of laws of nature implies that these are laws that operate independently of God. There are no such laws. There's only the providence of God acting in a common way and sometimes in a less common way.

There's indisputable evidence from the modern science of ethnology that such an event occurred as recorded in the book of Joshua. Chinese history speaks of Yao, their king, declaring that in his reign, the sun stood so long above the horizon that it was feared the world would be set on fire. History fixes the reign of Yao at the time of Joshua.[73] There's also evidence of legends of a long day scattered throughout the world.[74] Robert Boyd wrote:[75]

In the ancient Chinese writings there is a legend of a long day. The Incas of Peru and the Aztecs of Mexico have a like record. There is a Babylonian and Persian legend of a day that was miraculously extended. Herodotus, an ancient historian, recounts that while in Egypt, priests showed him their temple records, and that he read of a day which was twice the natural length of any day that had ever been recorded.

The Hermeneutical/Theological Debate

That's the philosophical debate, but there's another aspect to the debate. Some critics say that these words are poetic, that they are figurative instead of literal. Joshua, in a poetic way, was simply asking God for more strength. Joshua was saying, "God, help us to do two days' work in one day."

The argument goes something like this: Joshua was quoting poetry from the book of Jashar as a request to God for intervention in their battle, not a command to stop the sun's and the moon's motion in a literal sense.[76] The book of Jashar is a book of early Israelite poetry, a collection of national songs in honor of heroes.

Another version of this argument suggests that the inspired writer inserted this poetic account of the event into the narrative. Jamieson, Fausset, and Brown noted:[77]

The inspired author here breaks off the thread of his history of this miraculous victory to introduce a quotation from an ancient poem, in which the mighty acts of that day were commemorated. The passage, which is parenthetical, contains a poetical description of the victory which was miraculously gained by the help of God, and forms an extract from "the book of Jasher," that is, "the upright"—an anthology, or collection of national songs, in honor of renowned and eminently pious heroes.

If the words are poetic, then we shouldn't take what is described as literal. There was no long day. It's just a poetic rendering of the battle scene. Personally, I think it unlikely that General Joshua was up on a ridge quoting poetry while his army was fighting. This was a prayer request in the heat of battle. The answer to Joshua's prayer recorded in the very next verse indicates that the events were literal, not figurative.

> *And there was no day like that before it or after it, that the LORD hearkened unto the voice of a man: for the LORD fought for Israel.*
> *—Joshua 10:14*

The Jewish historian Josephus recorded the long day as a literal event when he noted:[78]

> Moreover, it happened that the day was lengthened, that the night might not come on too soon, and be an obstruction to the zeal of the Hebrews in pursuing their enemies; insomuch, that Joshua took the kings, who were hidden in a certain cave at Makkedah, and put them to death. Now, that the day was lengthened at this time, and was longer than ordinary, is expressed in the books laid up in the temple.

This was a literal solar event that had a worldwide impact. It was reported all over the world. The prophet Isaiah took it literally, warning that the God who proved His power at Gibeon on behalf of His people could turn that power against them in punishment!

For the LORD shall rise up as in mount Perazim, he shall be
wroth as in the valley of Gibeon, that he may do his work,
his strange work; and bring to pass his act, his strange act.
—Isaiah 28:21

Omen View

There's yet another view that says Joshua was just asking for a good omen. This approach considers the context of ancient Near Eastern culture, in which the movements of the sun, moon, stars, and planets were watched carefully as signs of good or bad omens. In this interpretation, there was no extraordinary interruption of the movement of heavenly bodies, only an alignment that could be taken as a good or evil omen.

One scholar proposed that Joshua's request was for a favorable sign for Israel, one in which both the sun and the moon would be visible at the same time: the sun rising and standing in the sky in the east before the moon had set in the west. The Canaanites would have seen this as an evil omen for themselves.[79]

Refreshment View

And there was no day like that before it or after it, that the
LORD hearkened unto the voice of a man: for the LORD

fought for Israel.

—Joshua 10:14

What if Joshua was simply asking for a release from the heat of the day, as some propose? Here they translate "stand still" to mean "be silent or leave off." Joshua was requesting that the sun cease from shining, and God answered that with a hailstorm. The problem with this idea is that the hailstorm came before Joshua's request in verse 12. Another view similar to this is offered by those who argue in favor of an eclipse. The great Old Testament scholar Robert Dick Wilson translated Joshua 10:12–14 as follows:[80]

> Be eclipsed, O sun, in Gibeon, and thou moon in the valley of Aijalon! And the sun was eclipsed and the moon turned back, while the nation was avenged on its enemies. Is it not written in the Book of Jasher? And the sun stayed in the half of the heaven, and set not hastily as when a day is done. And there was never a day like that day before or since, in respect to Jehovah's hearing the voice of a man.

Scripture states that this was something that had never happened before and has never happened since. That doesn't sound like refreshing from the sun because of an eclipse!

The Earth Stopped Revolving

Inexplicably, some say that the earth simply stopped revolving:[81]

> From Joshua's vantage point the sun stopped but we know that would mean that actually the earth stopped revolving. Those who argue for this view point to the fact that the text says that the sun stopped. The Hebrew uses two words daman and amad which have the idea "to stop." The word translated stand still (Hebrew dom) means literally to be silent and frequently has the sense cease or leave off (cf. Psalm 35:15; Lam. 2:18). Similarly the word translated stayed (Hebrew amad), stood still in v. 13b, has the sense of cease (cf. 2 Kings 4:6; Jonah 1:15). However, even if Joshua asked God to cause the sun "to stop" thus causing the earth to stop revolving that does not mean that this is what God did. This would have caused monstrous catastrophes all over the world.
>
> The earth revolves one time every 24 hours. A person standing at the equator would be circling the earth's axis at a speed of 1,035 miles an hour.

If you were on the hood of a car going 1,000 miles an hour and that car suddenly stopped on a dime, what would happen to you? If the earth had stopped, everything that wasn't nailed down would have been thrown into space, including Joshua and his army!

I believe the best explanation for what happened is that the earth slowed down its rotation. Notice the end of the passage: "So the sun stood still in the midst of heaven, and hasted not to go down about a whole day" (Joshua 10:13). The sun didn't hurry. Using the language of observation, it looked like the sun stood still, but the Bible says that it didn't hasten to go down. It slowed. It moved abnormally slowly. It crept across the sky, moving lethargically.

This would have given Joshua and the army of Israel more than enough daylight to win the battle over this confederacy of Canaanite kings without causing the universal catastrophic disturbances that would have happened if the earth had stopped rotating. Old Testament scholar Gleason Archer wrote:[82]

> It has been objected that if in fact the earth was stopped for a period of twenty-four hours, inconceivable catastrophe would have befallen the entire planet and everything on its surface. While those who believe in the omnipotence of God would hardly concede that Yahweh could not have prevented such catastrophe and held in abeyance the physical laws that might be brought to pass, it does not seem to be absolutely necessary (on the basis of the Hebrew text itself) to hold that the planet was suddenly halted in its rotation. Verse 13 states that the sun "did not hasten to go down for about a whole day" (NASB). The words "did not hasten" seem to point to a retardation of the movement so that the rotation required forty-eight hours rather than the usual twenty-four.

Donald K. Campbell agreed:[83]

> The best explanation seems to be the view that in answer to Joshua's prayer God caused the rotation of the earth to slow down so that it made one full rotation in 48 hours rather than in 24. It seems apparent that this view is supported by both the poem in verses 12b–13a and the prose in verse 13b.

In a syndicated AP article from May 8, 1973, the *Wisconsin State Journal* reported, "A giant storm on the sun last year probably slowed down the spinning of the earth for one rather long day." According to two scientists, this happened on August 4, 1972. "The length of day on any planet," the article concluded, "is governed by the time it takes to complete one full rotation. The faster it rotates, the shorter the day. So the earth must have slowed down fractionally."[84] Some people will read a story like that and believe it, yet they won't believe the Bible when God says this happened. From Joshua's vantage point, using the language of observation, the sun stood still. God answered his prayer, and He did it through an incredible miracle.

The Message of the Long Day

You may be thinking, *"All of this information is pretty cool, but how does it apply to me? I'm just trying to make it through the week. I just need strength to make it through this day."* The message of the long day is simply this: God fights for His people in profound ways. God gives victory to His people. God is the source of your victory. As I have said before, victory is not your responsibility; it's your response to His ability.

Here is the message in a sentence: The Lord gives victory, showing that He alone is Almighty God. God's Word is reliable. His promises are true. If God tells you something, He is going to do it. Even if He must move the heavens and the earth, God will do it. God performed this great miracle because He promised Joshua that not one of their enemies would be left standing at the end of the day.

Joshua said, "Lord, we need more light," and God replied, "No problem." God stopped the sun and the stars in their courses and did whatever was needed to fulfill His promise to His servant. His promises are true.

The Bible says, "Heaven and earth shall pass away: but my words shall not pass away" (Luke 21:33). I have no patience with those who attack the Word of God. Nevertheless, the Bible is like an anvil, and their attacks are like hammers. The hammers wear out, but the anvil remains intact. None of those attacks will ever stand. God didn't call preachers to be editors, but rather newsmen!

Position of Victory

There's a promise of victory, and then there's a position of victory. You may be thinking, *"I wish that God would fight for me the way He fought for Israel."* He will. You must position yourself for victory. You must be on God's side. You need to pray and to fill your mind with the Word. You need to profess that God never changes. He is the same today, tomorrow, and forever (Hebrews 13:8).

During the Civil War, many Americans in both the United States and the Confederate States believed God was on their side. According to one popular anecdote, a reporter asked President Lincoln, "Is God on your side?" Lincoln allegedly responded, "I am more concerned about whether or not I am on God's side." That should be our major concern! If you want victory in your life, you need to position yourself so you know that you are on God's side. If you are on God's side, those who fight against you are fighting against God, and they will surely fall like the Canaanite armies fell.

The Posture of Victory

When the Amorite kings ran from the battle, they hid themselves in a cave. Joshua told his men to roll stones in front of the cave and trap them inside. After the battle at Gibeon, Joshua rolled back the stones and brought out these five vanquished kings. Then he laid them in the dust and said to his captains, "Come near, put your feet upon the necks of these kings" (Joshua 10:24). Just picture that in your mind. Each captain came in turn and put his foot down, then waved his hands in victory. Joshua did that as an object lesson for all of Israel: "This is what God will do to all your enemies!"

> *And Joshua said unto them, Fear not, nor be dismayed, be strong and of good courage: for thus shall the LORD do to all your enemies against whom ye fight.*
> *—Joshua 10:25*

This was the posture of victory. The Israelites might still have been a little fearful, and this calmed them. They had their feet on the necks of these kings. They were in control of the situation. The kings weren't going anywhere.

Jesus is our Joshua. Jesus lays Satan low in the dust. He says to Christians, to you and me, "Come here and put your foot on his neck. Put your foot there." You don't need to worry about your enemy because God has already won the battle. This is the posture of total victory. Satan is a defeated foe. When Jesus predicted His death on the cross, He said, "...now shall the prince of this world be cast out" (John 12:31). Remember that victory is not your destination; it's your point of origin. The next time the devil tries to scare you, just picture him lying in the dust with your foot on his neck in victory through Jesus Christ, our Joshua.

The Preview of Victory

And afterward Joshua smote them, and slew them, and hanged them on five trees: and they were hanging upon the trees until the evening. And it came to pass at the time of the going down of the sun, that Joshua commanded, and they took them down off the trees, and cast them into the cave wherein they had been hid, and laid great stones in the cave's mouth, which remain until this very day.
—Joshua 10:26–27

The Israelites hung their enemies on trees to show that they were cursed by God. When I read this, I can't help but think of another king who hung on a tree, the Lord Jesus Christ. He was the sinless Son of God. He did nothing worthy of death, but He took on the curse of disobedience of the law, my sin and yours. Paul referred to this in Galatians when he wrote:

Christ hath redeemed us from the curse of the law, being made a curse for us: for it is written, Cursed is every one that hangeth on a tree....
—Galatians 3:13

Did you know that every individual born of Adam is under a curse? Where did that curse come from? A few verses earlier in Galatians, Paul wrote, "Cursed is every one that continueth not in all things which are written in the book of the law to do them" (Galatians 3:10). This curse comes from disobeying God's law.

Some people believe they are able to gain their eternal salvation through good works and religious rituals. This is the very idea Paul was refuting. False teachers came to the region of Galatia after Paul left and taught believers there that salvation was faith plus obeying the law with all its religious rituals. Paul was reminding the believers at Galatia that the law doesn't save. It has no power to save; it can only condemn.

If people endeavor to earn their salvation by obedience to the law, then they must obey every part of the law perfectly. Anything less than absolute perfection brings the curse of the law on the transgressor. Since no person born of Adam's fallen race has obeyed the law perfectly, everyone is under the curse.

The good news, however, is that Christ came to redeem us from the curse of the law. How? He became a curse for us. This is hard to fathom. Many Jews in Paul's day, and perhaps even today, struggled over the idea that God's Messiah would be cursed by being hung on a tree.

In Galatians 3:13, Paul quoted Deuteronomy 21:23:

His body shall not remain all night upon the tree, but thou shalt in any wise bury him that day; (for he that is hanged is accursed of God;) that thy land be not defiled, which the LORD thy God giveth thee for an inheritance.

The Jews didn't crucify criminals. They stoned them and then hung them on trees as a public display to show others that these people were cursed by God. This was commanded by God in Deuteronomy 21:22:

And if a man have committed a sin worthy of death, and he be to be put to death, and thou hang him on a tree....

The body wasn't allowed to stay overnight because that would have been an offense to God. The Israelites took these regulations seriously. After Joshua's army defeated the small city of Ai, the king of Ai was killed and hung on a tree as the law required, but he was taken down at sunset in obedience to God's law (Joshua 8:29).

After God gave Joshua this miraculous victory over the five kings of the Amorites, Joshua took them from the cave where he had trapped them until he had finished defeating their forces, and he killed them. Joshua then hung all five of them on trees, but he took them down at sunset in order to comply with God's law (Joshua 10:26–27).

When Jesus died on the rugged tree, the cross, the Jewish leaders made sure to get Him down from the cross before sunset (John 19:31) so as not to desecrate the Sabbath. This shows that they believed Jesus was cursed by God. To the Jews, hanging on a tree was the ultimate curse! That's why they didn't believe Jesus was the Messiah. They couldn't imagine that God would allow His Messiah to die on a tree and be a curse. They didn't understand that the reason Jesus died was to remove the curse of the law. The message of Christianity was offensive to the Jews because at the center of it was a man hanging and dying on a tree. The message was about a man who was so cursed by God that he was crucified. Even so, the apostles didn't try to hide this fact, but rather drew attention to it. When Peter preached to the Jewish leaders in Jerusalem, he said:

> *The God of our fathers raised up Jesus, whom ye slew and hanged on a tree.*
>
> —*Acts 5:30*

> *Who his own self bare our sins in his own body on the tree, that we, being dead to sins, should live unto righteousness: by whose stripes ye were healed.*
>
> —*1 Peter 2:24*

When Paul spoke in the synagogue at Pisidian Antioch, he described how Jesus was taken down from the tree (Acts 13:29). The Apostles almost went out of their way to call the cross a tree, yet at the same time, they claimed that the crucified Jesus was the Christ. To the Jew, this was absolute blasphemy: a cursed Messiah on a cursed cross. No wonder the cross was a stumbling block to them!

Perhaps Paul struggled with this himself before his own conversion. After Paul met Jesus on the Damascus road, God revealed to Paul the resolution to the dilemma of why God would allow the Messiah to die on a tree. In order to redeem mankind from the curse of the law, He had to become a curse: "Christ hath redeemed us from the curse of the law, being made a curse for us" (Galatians 3:13).

How did Christ redeem us from the curse? How did He become a curse? To sum it up in one word: obedience. Mankind's disobedience brought the curse, and Christ's obedience removed it. Systematic theologians like to make a distinction between the active obedience of Christ and His passive obedience. Active obedience is when Jesus fulfilled all of the law of God on our behalf. He fulfilled all the moral demands of God's law. The active obedience refers to His whole life of obeying the law of God, whereby He qualifies to be the Savior. He qualifies to be the Lamb without blemish.

Through His total righteousness, He qualifies for the song with the lyrics "Worthy is the Lamb who was slain."[85] He fulfills the law's demands, and according to the covenant with Moses, everybody who fulfills the law receives the blessing, but those who disobey the law receive the curse. Not only did Jesus have to die for our sins, but He also had to live for our righteousness.

Passive obedience is when Jesus submitted Himself to death on the cross. He submitted Himself to suffer and die for our sins. The passive obedience of Christ refers to His willingness to endure the pain that was inflicted upon Him by the Father on the cross in the atonement. He passively received the curse of God. God's holiness demands that the curse of sin be punished. God's love doesn't want to punish you. God's plan was to send His Son, Jesus, to bear the curse of sin in your place.

Galatians 3:13 says that Christ was "made a curse *for* us" (emphasis added). Jesus bore this real curse, the curse of the law, the curse of sin, the curse of God's wrath. The curse that was upon us was placed on Him. The Greek word translated as *for* is not the normal Greek word *gar*, but rather the word *hyper*, which means, "in place of, on behalf of, or for the sake of."[86] Christ became a curse in place of us for our sakes.

No wonder Jesus said when on the cross, "My God, my God, why hast thou forsaken me?" (Matthew 27:46). Jesus was bearing the curse. He had become a curse for us. In the old, rugged cross, we see the wrath of God against sin, the curse of the broken law, the Son being accursed by the Father on our behalf. It boggles the mind! Jesus endured God's curse to save us. It reminds me of the words of the old American folk hymn:[87]

> What wondrous love is this,
> O my soul, O my soul
> What wondrous love is this,
> O my soul!
> What wondrous love is this,
> That caused the Lord of bliss
> To bear the dreadful curse
> For my soul, for my soul,
> To bear the dreadful curse for my soul!

Imagine that you were millions of dollars in financial debt. A certain rich man decided he was going to pay your debt, so he paid it all. All your financial debts were paid, but you still had nothing. Then this same rich man decided that on top of paying your debt, he would also add millions of dollars to your account. He was so wealthy and kind that he not only paid your debt, but also made you wealthy by adding millions to your account!

What would you think of someone who did that for

you? Jesus *did* do that for you in a spiritual sense. With His passive obedience, He paid your sin debt. And with His active obedience, He added righteousness to your account, so you are now righteous before God when you put your faith in His finished work.

When I read of the five kings of the Amorites being hung on trees and bearing the curse of the law in a public display, I can't help but think of the Messiah and Savior Jesus, who became a curse for you and me. Even in the names of these kings, I see glimpses of the Christ of Calvary.

Prophetic Names of the Amorite Kings

Adoni-zedek means "Lord of righteousness."[88] This man was the king of Jerusalem. There's only one Lord of righteousness who is the King of Jerusalem, and that's Jesus. One day He will return and reign in righteousness from the throne of David in Jerusalem.

Hohman is the name of another king, and it means "alas, he crushed."[89] That reminds me of Jesus, the King who crushed Satan at Calvary. Jesus crushes our enemies for us (Genesis 3:15 NIV).

Piram means "to divide" or "to separate."[90] Jesus is the real King who divides and separates because when you choose to follow Jesus, you have to separate from the world. When you choose to side with Jesus, you will automatically divide from other things and people.

Japhia means "to rise" or "to shine,"[91] and that

reminds me of how, after being the sin-bearer who was hung on a tree, Jesus rose. He was the glory of God robed in human flesh, and every once in a while in the Gospels, we see a glimpse of the glory of God shining forth in Christ. When He returns one day, it will be in clouds of glory.

Debir is a Hebrew word that means "oracle" or "word."[9293] Jesus is the King who is the Word. He is the Word of God, and God speaks to us through Him.

The Tomb

They laid these kings in a tomb, and the Bible says that they remained there "until this very day" (Joshua 10:27). Jesus was laid in a tomb, but He didn't stay there. Three days later, He rose and came out!

This long day of fighting for Joshua and the nation of Israel ended. Eventually, the sun did set. This long day called life that you are in right now is also going to end one day, but there's power in the resurrection to extend your day into eternity, contrary to all the so-called "laws of nature." You can walk and live in the power of the cross and the power of the Lord Jesus Christ!

WORKBOOK

Chapter Eight Questions

Question: How did Joshua model integrity in his response to the Gibeonites? Why would this have been difficult? Describe a relationship in which it's challenging for you to walk in integrity. How might God reward you for doing so?

_____

_____

_____

_____

_____

_____

_____

_____

_____

Question: What are some things that the Bible says are the will of God for every believer? How are you doing with obeying those commands? Is your love for Christ evidenced by your obedience? (See John 14:15 and 1 John 5:3.)

_____

_____

_____

_____

_____

_____

_____

_____

_____

Journal: Have you ever asked God for a miracle? Is there a situation you are facing now that seems impossible? How is God fighting for you right now? How do you already have the victory, and in what ways do you need to realize the victory you have been given?

_____

_____

_____

_____

_____

_____

_____

_____

_____

_____

Action: Draw or create a graphic with a picture of the sun and the moon. Write the word *victory* and place your sign where it will be a reminder to you that God fights for you and promises victory.

Chapter Eight Notes

CHAPTER NINE

I Want That Mountain
Joshua 14:1–15

Big Idea: *In order to claim our spiritual inheritance, we must be willing to take on difficult challenges by faith.*

On May 29, 1953, Edmond Hillary reached the summit of Mount Everest at about 11:30 in the morning.[9495] At the age of 33, Hillary conquered the highest mountain on earth. Many before him had attempted to do the same but failed. In March 1953, when the expedition set out, it included about four hundred people. During the attempt, the crew experienced severe snow and wind, which often delayed their travel.

Climbers were broken up into teams, and Hillary was paired up with Tenzing Norgay. The trip up the mountain was extremely difficult, and when the teams neared the summit, only four were able to continue. One by one, the remaining teams dropped out until only Hillary and

Norgay were able to continue and successfully reach the summit. Hillary would go on to face many great challenges in life, but I believe God helped him through them all.

The church today needs dedicated men and women for God, people who are willing—no, *eager*—to conquer seemingly impossible mountains. Where are those men and women who are willing to take on difficult challenges for the glory of God? They are the kind needed to carry the gospel into this twenty-first-century world.

I want to introduce to you one of God's hard men, one of God's men who was not afraid of treacherous mountains: Caleb, the gray-haired conqueror.

Now therefore give me this mountain, whereof the LORD spake in that day; for thou heardest in that day how the Anakims were there, and that the cities were great and fenced: if so be the LORD will be with me, then I shall be able to drive them out, as the LORD said.
—Joshua 14:12

Claiming the Land

Joshua's assignment was complete, but Israel's job was just beginning. Joshua broke the back of the military strongholds. The kings were all routed and defeated. That opened up the land for the twelve tribes to begin driving out the Canaanites in their territories.

Now Joshua was old and stricken in years; and the LORD said unto him, Thou art old and stricken in years, and there

remaineth yet very much land to be possessed.
                                    —Joshua 13:1

In Joshua 11–12, we have the record of Joshua's conquest of the rest of the land of Canaan. Joshua led three major military campaigns in Canaan: the northern, central, and southern campaigns. The Bible records that Joshua took the whole land:

> *And they smote all the souls that were therein with the edge of the sword, utterly destroying them: there was not any left to breathe: and he burnt Hazor with fire. And all the cities of those kings, and all the kings of them, did Joshua take, and smote them with the edge of the sword, and he utterly destroyed them, as Moses the servant of the LORD commanded.*
> *—Joshua 11:11–12*

> *So Joshua took the whole land, according to all that the LORD said unto Moses; and Joshua gave it for an inheritance unto Israel according to their divisions by their tribes. And the land rested from war.*
> *—Joshua 11:23*

This may seem confusing as you read the book of Joshua. If Joshua conquered all the land, why does it later say that some tribes failed to drive out the Canaanites? It's important to distinguish between the work Joshua had to do and the work the individual tribes of Israel had left to do. Joshua's job was completed! Canaan had been conquered. Its standing armies had been routed. Its principal strongholds had been destroyed. Its mighty kings had been slain.

Chapter 12 contains a list of kings and strongholds that Joshua conquered (Joshua 12:7–24), yet much of the actual territory was in the hands of its original inhabitants. The backs of the Canaanites had been broken. Now the individual tribes had to go in and do the mopping-up operation. Since the military strongholds had been taken and the Canaanite kings had been defeated, there was nothing to stop them from taking full possession. Chapter 13 opens up with the challenge for the individual tribes to do their part in driving out and clearing out the inhabitants of the land.

What does all of this mean for believers today? Israel had to take possession of what God had given them, but that didn't mean there wouldn't be any battles. On the cross, Jesus defeated Satan. Satan's back was broken, and his head was crushed, but that doesn't mean you, as a Christian, won't have battles against Satan. All he can do is rattle his cage and try to scare you. He can't harm you if you are a child of God, but you still have to claim the victory the Lord gave you. This is what happened with Israel.

Caleb's Claim

In Chapter 13, God, the divine realtor, began to divide the land and assign lots to tribes. In Chapter 14, as Joshua was giving out land, a familiar face showed up. Caleb was one of the generation of Jews who left Egypt. He was there when God sent plagues upon Egypt, he was there when God divided the Red Sea, and he was one of the twelve spies who originally went into the promised land. Ten of the spies had a bad report, but Joshua and Caleb said, "We can do it!" Caleb saw the miracles of God. He believed in the power of God, but because of the unbelieving Jews, he had to wait forty years to enter the promised land.

When Caleb came back from his sortie into the promised land, Moses commended him for his faith and courage:

> *And Moses sware on that day, saying, Surely the land whereon thy feet have trodden shall be thine inheritance, and thy children's for ever, because thou hast wholly followed the LORD my God.*
>
> —*Joshua 14:9*

Now that Joshua was giving out lots, Caleb reminded him of Moses' promise in case Joshua had forgotten. Caleb wanted that mountain God had promised to give him. He requested the same land that had struck fear into the hearts of the ten unbelieving spies. This was the inheritance he desired. Mount Hebron was one of the toughest sections still to be overcome, full of fortified cities and the Anakim giants. Caleb was eighty-five years old. Though old age is usually a time when people are more eager to talk about old battles than to take on new ones, Caleb was ready and eager for one more good fight!

The simple story is this: Caleb did exactly what he said he was going to do. He took that mountain and drove out the Canaanites. He drove out the giants.

Claiming Your Inheritance

How does this narrative apply to your life? Joshua is an image of Jesus, our conqueror. Just as Joshua won the victory for Israel, Jesus won the victory for us. Caleb is an image of the believer who came to Joshua to claim his inheritance. As a believer, you have to go to Jesus to claim your inheritance. What is the mountain the Lord has promised you? You need to go and claim it. You need to say, "It's mine by faith. I claim it. I'm going to take it."

When I read this narrative, I can't help but think of the church I now have the privilege to pastor. Grace Bible Baptist Church was started by my own pastor, Dr. Earl M. Johnson, Jr. I learned much about living a life of faith by sitting under his ministry. He exemplified a Caleb-like spirit more than any other person I have ever known.

Our church campus sits on land that Pastor Johnson claimed by faith when he and a small handful of people had zero money to purchase it. During the time when they were praying and asking God to give them the land, the congregation would sing the hymn "I Want That Mountain" in their worship services. God did indeed give them the land and so many blessings with it.

In all the years Pastor Johnson led the congregation at Grace, mountain-size challenges would arise. Each time a new challenge presented itself, Pastor Johnson would face it with a Caleb-like faith, singing, "I want that mountain!" Pastor Johnson is in heaven now, but I, along with the congregation of Grace, continue to reap the benefits of victories he won by faith.

Now that I am the Senior Pastor at Grace and face some

of the same challenges he did, I try to emulate the courageous faith he demonstrated. We all face imposing mountains inhabited by giants on our spiritual journeys. Caleb modeled for us the kind of courageous faith we need in order to surmount them and claim our inheritance.

And the name of Hebron before was Kirjatharba; which Arba was a great man among the Anakims. And the land had rest from war.

—Joshua 14:15

Caleb changed the name of the city of Kirjath Arba (NKJV) to Hebron, which means "seat of association" or "seat of fellowship."[96] I admire the fact that Caleb didn't name the city after himself as Arba had done. That tells me a lot about the heart of Caleb. He desired fellowship with God. To him, that mountain represented fellowship. Then the land had a break from war.

Fellowship

One of the greatest blessings of your salvation is fellowship with Jesus. When you, as a child of God, go to heaven and meet Jesus, you won't meet a stranger. You will meet someone face to face whom you have known heart to heart. The fellowship you have with Jesus is so very real. The Apostle John described fellowship with Jesus in the following way:

That which was from the beginning, which we have heard, which we have seen with our eyes, which we have looked

upon, and our hands have handled, of the Word of life; (For
the life was manifested, and we have seen it, and bear wit-
ness, and shew unto you that eternal life, which was with
the Father, and was manifested unto us;) That which we
have seen and heard declare we unto you, that ye also may
have fellowship with us: and truly our fellowship is with
the Father, and with his Son Jesus Christ.

—1 John 1:1–3

When I travel to Israel to do archaeological digs, I have
a favorite place I love to visit. I always make it a point to
travel to northern Israel, to the Sea of Galilee, to see the
places where Jesus walked. I visit the little village of Capernaum. That's where Jesus set up His headquarters
during His earthly ministry. One can still see the remains
of a beautiful little village right there on the Sea of Galilee.

The basalt stone foundation of the first synagogue is
still there. This would have been the synagogue where Jesus taught many of the things we read of in the Gospels.
Archaeologists have uncovered there what they believe is
the house of Peter. When I walk through the remains of
this sacred place, I imagine what it would have been like
to be there with Jesus, to see Him, to hear Him, to fellowship with Him. John was there at Capernaum with Jesus
and experienced real fellowship with Him. He heard Him,
saw His miracles, and studied at His feet. What an incredible experience that was for John!

Even though it's always wonderful to visit Capernaum,
the truth is that we don't have to go there to experience
real fellowship with Jesus. John was teaching us that any
child of God can have fellowship with Christ that's just as

spiritually real and rich as the fellowship he had with Jesus at Capernaum and around the Sea of Galilee. John was saying, "We heard Him. We saw Him. We touched Him. The other disciples and I enjoyed fellowship with Jesus, and you can have that same fellowship. It can be just as real." John wrote these things "that your joy may be full" (1 John 1:4).

Fullness

That mountain also represents fullness. The area Caleb conquered was the lushest, most beautiful area in that land, and Caleb didn't just conquer half of it. He conquered all of it! That's a picture of the Christian getting all that God has for each of us. I don't want half of Hebron; I want the fullness of all that God has for me. In the New Testament, Paul prayed that believers would come to understand and experience the fullness of God (Ephesians 3:19; 4:13).

Fruitfulness

This is the very place where the spies took grapes to bring back to the Israelites to show them how lush and fruitful the land was (Numbers 13:22–27). This mountain represents fruitfulness. I want the fruit of the Spirit in my life. I want to be fruitful as a Christian, so I want to say, as Caleb did, "Now therefore give me this mountain" (Joshua 14:12).

202 · JERRY HARMON

Caleb's Character

Let me give you three of Caleb's qualities that you
need to have in your life if you want that mountain.

Commitment

Take a few minutes to read the verses below in your
Bible:

- Numbers 14:24

- Numbers 32:12

- Deuteronomy 1:36

- Joshua 14: 8–9, 14

The phrase you will see over and over about Caleb is
that he "wholly followed the LORD." Caleb was totally
committed. What does it mean to follow the Lord wholly?
That phrase means "to close the gap."[97] Caleb kept the
distance between himself and the Lord at a minimum. If
you want to be a Canaanite conqueror and not a wilderness wanderer, then you must wholly follow the Lord.

Many Christians have one foot in the church and one
foot in the world. They maintain an escape hatch back to
the old life of sin. If you live like that, you will never be
blessed of God and you will never have the mountain you
long for. You need to burn every bridge that leads back to
the old life and set your mind on conquering your Canaan!

Jim Elliot, a missionary whose life was taken by

indigenous warriors in Ecuador in the mid-twentieth century, wrote, "He is no fool who gives up what he cannot keep to gain what he cannot lose."[98]

In *Basic Christian: The Inside Story of John Stott*, Roger Steer gave the following account of a letter Stott received from Leslie Weatherhead:

> Soon after the publication of John Stott's 1971 revised edition of Basic Christian, he received a letter that read:
>
> *Dear John,*
>
> *Thank you for writing Basic Christianity. It led me to make a new commitment of my life to Christ. I am old now—nearly 78—but not too old to make a new beginning.*
>
> *I rejoice in all the grand work you are doing.*
>
> *Yours sincerely,*
> *Leslie Weatherhead*
>
> Leslie Weatherhead was one of the most respected and influential Christian leaders in the United Kingdom. Thousands heard him preach at City Temple, his books were read widely, he pioneered in the field of pastoral counseling, and he was president of the Methodist Conference. Yet at 78-years-old he was not too proud or too worn out to make a fresh commitment of his life.[99]

May the same be said of us. The key to usefulness in God's kingdom is our commitment to Him.

Confidence

The apologist Ravi Zacharias wrote, "Faith is confidence in the person of Jesus Christ and in his power, so

that even when his power does not serve my end, my confidence in him remains because of who he is."[100] Caleb
always clung to what the Lord said to him. Caleb had confidence, but his confidence was not in himself. When God
said something, Caleb knew he could depend on it. In fact,
he inferred that the reason he was so strong and in such
good shape at his age was because of the Lord.

> And now, behold, the LORD hath kept me alive, as he said,
> these forty and five years, even since the LORD spake this
> word unto Moses, while the children of Israel wandered in
> the wilderness: and now, lo, I am this day fourscore and
> five years old.
> —*Joshua 14:10*

Caleb found the secret of youthful strength. He said,
"I'm as strong now as I was when I was 40" (Joshua
14:11, paraphrased). He was trusting in the Lord. He was
trusting in the promises of God. The God who reserves the
promise for the man is the God who reserves the man for
the promise. Caleb said, "Now therefore give me this
mountain" (Joshua 14:12), because he was confident in
the promises of God. He had faith.

- Faith is not positive thinking.
- Faith is not optimism.
- Faith is not looking on the bright side.
- Faith is simply acting on what God says.

I can see Caleb climbing that mountain with a sword in one hand and a title deed in the other. Caleb knew God had given it to him, so he took it.

Courage

Even if you wholly follow the Lord, you will still have challenges. The Christian life is not the absence of problems, but the addition of God's power to handle those problems. There's no easy way to serve God, and Caleb had challenges.

First of all, there's the problem of grasshoppers. These are people who are focused on their circumstances and not focused on the Lord. You will always have grasshoppers around you, telling you that something can't be done when God is saying that you can do it! You must "walk by faith, not by sight" (2 Corinthians 5:7). Someone who walks by sight will see a difficulty in every opportunity. A person who walks by faith will see an opportunity in every difficulty. Caleb had to wait to inherit the promised land because of the giant Anakim, but by faith and patience, he overcame them.

Caleb wasn't afraid of the giants. He knew they were there, but he said, "If God is with me, I can drive them out" (Joshua 14:12, paraphrased). In the Christian life, you will have giants you must face. They may be giants of disease, disappointment, depression, addiction, financial reversal, career setback, family breakdown, or personal failure. We all have giants.

And Caleb drove thence the three sons of Anak, Sheshai,
and Ahiman, and Talmai, the children of Anak.
—*Joshua 15:14*

Sheshai means "who I am," Ahiman means "what I am," and Talmai means "what I can do." These are the giants of ego, pride, and self-reliance. You also must overcome the giants of your flesh that live inside you—your ego, pride, and self-reliance—if you are going to follow God wholeheartedly.[101]

Caleb wasn't a young man, but he didn't let age keep him from doing the will of God. At 85, he said, "I want that mountain!" He trusted the Lord, and God gave it to him. Caleb overcame all obstacles, and he kept doing what the Lord wanted him to do. No matter what his age was, God had put something on his heart. God will also keep you alive as long as you need to be to fulfill all that He has planned for you. You can count on it.

Chapter Nine Questions

Question: Have you ever thought that you were too old to serve God in a particular way or to make a difference for His kingdom? What are some of the advantages that a seasoned servant of God has over a new believer? What are some dangers that can come with the familiarity of many years of ministry and leadership? Where should your confidence lie, regardless of your age?

_____

_____

_____

_____

_____

_____

_____

_____

_____

_____

_____

Question: Would others say of you that you wholly follow the Lord, as was said of Caleb? Where are there gaps in your relationship with Christ, and how can you close them?

_____

_____

_____

_____

_____

_____

_____

_____

_____

Journal: What is the "mountain" of fellowship, fullness, and fruitfulness God has for your life? What is hindering you from each of these? How will you step forward and claim the inheritance Jesus Christ has already won for you and promised to you?

_____

_____

_____

_____

_____

_____

_____

_____

_____

_____

_____

Action: Print or draw an image of a mountain. Within the mountain, list the various promises God has made to you in His Word or straight to your heart. Commit to praying regularly over each of those promises, "It's mine by faith. I claim it. I'm going to take it."

Chapter Nine Notes

CHAPTER TEN

Failing to Possess Your Possessions
Joshua 17:12–18; 18:1–3

Big Idea: Sins we have failed to put to death in our lives prevent us from fully enjoying the blessings of our spiritual inheritance.

Years ago, a dear Christian man and member of our church bought me an expensive computer software program. When I say expensive, I mean expensive. This was the newest tool for anyone who wanted to study Scripture on a deep level. The program offered all kinds of tools and study aids. It also included a vast library of the best commentaries and monographs on diverse theological topics. The gift was overwhelming, and not being very computer literate at that time, I didn't fully comprehend what had been given to me. In order to use this program to the fullest, I had to be diligent and learn how to operate it.

To my shame, I didn't do that. The program was set aside, and I went on doing things the old way. Imagine my surprise when I would buy a set of commentaries or a valuable book, only to find out later that I already had those volumes on my software program! It wasn't until I took some workshops and learned how to utilize the program that I began to realize the treasure I had been given. Study and preparation became so much easier and more rewarding. My problem was that I failed to possess what I had been given to the fullest. As we come to chapter 17 of the book of Joshua, this is the plight of several of the tribes of Israel.

Joshua was from the tribe of Ephraim, and Shiloh was right in the center of the promised land, so Joshua set up the tabernacle in Shiloh. All that was left to be done was for the children of Israel, the various tribes, to settle their inheritance and further drive out the Canaanites.

Inadvisably, some of the tribes of Israel chose not to drive out all the Canaanites and fully possess the land. Joshua addressed this problem:

> *And the whole congregation of the children of Israel assembled together at Shiloh, and set up the tabernacle of the congregation there. And the land was subdued before them. And there remained among the children of Israel seven tribes, which had not yet received their inheritance. And Joshua said unto the children of Israel, How long are ye slack to go to possess the land, which the Lord God of your fathers hath given you?*
>
> *—Joshua 18:1–3*

This was an ominous problem that one could see coming. The writer alluded to it several times leading up to chapter 17. In Joshua 15:63, we read, "As for the Jebusites the inhabitants of Jerusalem, the children of Judah could not drive them out; but the Jebusites dwell with the children of Judah at Jerusalem unto this day." Similarly, the Ephraimites "drave not out the Canaanites that dwelt in Gezer: but the Canaanites dwell among the Ephraimites unto this day, and serve under tribute" (Joshua 16:10). Joshua 17:12 tells us that "the children of Manasseh could not drive out the inhabitants of those cities; but the Canaanites would dwell in that land."

A. W. Pink called these tribes "sad blemishes" in light of the fact that the nation of Israel enjoyed general success.[102] There were some tribes that simply were not possessing their possession. As we examine this narrative, we can see several reasons why the tribes were failing to drive out the Canaanites.

Pride

> *And the children of Joseph spake unto Joshua, saying, Why hast thou given me but one lot and one portion to inherit, seeing I am a great people, forasmuch as the LORD hath blessed me hitherto?*
>
> **—Joshua 17:14**

The same people who couldn't drive out the Canaanites and who failed to possess the land they already had were asking for more land. The moment you think you deserve more than what God has given you, you are deceived.

Manasseh's pride was probably based on the fact that their ancestor, Joseph, had been second to Pharaoh. They thought his glory was reflected on them. Throughout the Old Testament, you will find that the Israelites were given to pride and criticism. They were prone to complaining, and Moses and Joshua frequently had to correct their attitude.

Joshua answered these people, and I think there's a strong note of irony, maybe even sarcasm, in his words. He said, "If you're such a great people, then take care of business. Clear the forest, clear the wood, and then you'll have all the land you need. Take care of what you have before asking for more land. Take care of what you have already been given" (Joshua 17:15–18, paraphrased).

The bottom line is that their pride was hindering them from doing their duty. You are never more like the devil than when you walk in pride. Remember that in Joshua 15, Caleb had to chase away three giants—Sheshai ("who I am"), Ahiman ("what I am") and Talmai ("what I can do")—which remind us of our own giants of ego, pride, and self-reliance.[103] Before you have victory, you must drive out those giants in your life. When people become focused on self and neglect to cast themselves before the Lord in humble dependence, they are on dangerous ground. Pride will keep you from reaching your full potential for God. God hates pride: "But he giveth more grace. Wherefore he saith, God resisteth the proud, but giveth grace unto the humble" (James 4:6).

Procrastination

How long are ye slack to go to possess the land, which the
LORD God of your fathers hath given you?

—*Joshua 18:3*

Joshua was reprimanding these tribes for their procrastination. The Israelites had become accustomed to a nomadic lifestyle, and they weren't anxious to do the work of settling. It was easier to wait around, so they sat idle and did nothing. Sound familiar? You may not think procrastination is sin, but it is a sin if God has told you to do something. The Bible says, "Therefore to him that knoweth to do good, and doeth it not, to him it is sin" (James 4:17). Procrastination is dangerous. What if you miss a great God-given opportunity? What if a loved one fails to hear the gospel because you procrastinated? If you study church history, you will find that the saints who were greatly used by God weren't given to idleness or procrastination.

In 1865, Charles Spurgeon launched a magazine called *The Sword and the Trowel*, in which he regularly included maxims under the pen name John Ploughman. The character was actually based on an old farmer, Will Richardson, in Spurgeon's hometown of Stambourne. As a boy, Spurgeon spent many an hour in the furrows behind Richardson's plow, listening to the man's homespun quips, quotes, comments, and common sense. Years later, in his garden house where *The Sword and the Trowel* was edited, Spurgeon's mind wandered back to those scenes as he composed Ploughman's proverbs.[104] When the proverbs were collected and issued as *John Ploughman's Talks,* it became his bestselling book.

The first chapter of *John Ploughman's Talks* is entitled "To the Idle." Among many maxims, the Ploughman wrote:[105]

- The rankest weeds on earth don't grow in the minds of those who are busy at wickedness, but in foul corners of idle men's imaginations, where the devil can hide away unseen like an old serpent as he is.

- Idle men tempt the devil to tempt them.

- The Lord Jesus tells us himself that when men slept the enemy sowed the tares; and that hits the nail on the head, for it is by the door of sluggishness that evil enters the heart more often, it seems to me, than by any other.

Joshua's rebuke of these idle tribes was necessary and right. We also need to be reminded that we are missing out on enjoying the spiritual benefits of our inheritance in Christ if we are not diligent in the spiritual disciplines of prayer, Bible study, meditation, and worship.

Presumption

Yet the children of Manasseh could not drive out the inhabitants of those cities; but the Canaanites would dwell in that land. Yet it came to pass, when the children of Israel

*were waxen strong, that they put the Canaanites to trib-
ute, but did not utterly drive them out.*
—*Joshua 17:12–13*

To *presume* means "to speak or act without warrant or proudly."[106] This exactly describes the actions of the children of Manasseh. Ultimately, they decided that they had a better plan than God's. Interestingly, verse 12 says that they *could not* drive out the Canaanites, and verse 13 indicates that they *would not* drive them out. At first, they didn't think they were strong enough to drive them out. Then, when they knew they were strong enough, they decided not to do it. The plan shifted to use the Canaanites for the tribe's benefit. They decided to use them as servants and make them pay taxes.

The children of Manasseh probably got this idea from Joshua and the elders of Israel. Do you remember how Joshua and the elders of Israel made an unwise decision and entered into a peace treaty with the Gibeonites instead of driving them out? The Gibeonites pretended to be from a far country, and rather than thoroughly vetting them, Joshua and the elders believed their deception. When they realized they were deceived, Joshua and the elders decided to make these Canaanites serve them (Joshua 9).

Now the children of Manasseh were doing the same thing. Perhaps they thought, "If Joshua did it, then why can't we?" It's funny how we can always find a reason to justify our disobedience. Their presumption, however, would come to haunt the nation of Israel.

We must be careful never to presume upon the grace of God in our lives by replacing His Word with our own desires. David prayed, "Keep back thy servant also from presumptuous sins; let them not have dominion over me" (Psalm 19:13).

Keeping Company with Canaanites

The children of Manasseh decided it was better to keep company with the Canaanites than to drive them out. For the purpose of our study, the Canaanites represent the power of sin in the life of the believer. God told Israel to drive the Canaanites out of the land completely. In fact, Joshua warned the children of Israel just before he was about to die:

> *Else if ye do in any wise go back, and cleave unto the remnant of these nations, even these that remain among you, and shall make marriages with them, and go in unto them, and they to you: Know for a certainty that the LORD your God will no more drive out any of these nations from before you; but they shall be snares and traps unto you, and scourges in your sides, and thorns in your eyes, until ye perish from off this good land which the LORD your God hath given you.*
> *—Joshua 23:12–13*

This is a strict warning from Joshua to deal thoroughly with the Canaanites. If the Israelites failed to do so, they would come to regret it. The Canaanites would become, among other things, snares and thorns in Israel's eyes.

Similarly, Jesus warned us to be merciless with personal sin, which robs us of victory and blessing. He said, "If thy right eye offend thee, pluck it out, and cast it from thee" (Matthew 5:29). He continued, "And if thy right hand offend thee, cut it off, and cast it from thee" (Matthew 5:30). Jesus wasn't being literal here. He wasn't calling for self-mutilation of the body, but rather mortification of the sins of the soul. He was using hyperbole to emphasize the vital lesson that one must be merciless in killing sin. Sin, like Canaanites, not dealt with thoroughly will rise up to conquer us one day.

God's plan for Manasseh was total victory. However, they didn't achieve it because of the Canaanites around them. There were Canaanites whom Manasseh favored and chose not to drive out. Some Christians today are keeping company with "Canaanites"—accepted sins or pet sins. Some may choose not to drive out those sins because they are familiar and seem harmless, but you must drive them out if you want to achieve your full potential in Christ.

There were also Canaanites whom Manasseh feared and thought they couldn't overcome. Since they thought they couldn't overcome them, they didn't even try. There may be sins you consider too difficult to drive out of your life. That's a lie of the devil. If you are a Christian and the Holy Spirit of God lives inside of you, there is no sin in your life that you cannot overcome with His power.

In the book of Judges, the Canaanite slaves left in the land of Israel rose up in rebellion. The plan to gain materially from the Canaanites backfired. Likewise, the sins you enjoy today will come back to trouble you tomorrow. They will rise up and master you. Deal thoroughly with your sins, or your sins will deal thoroughly with you!

Killing Canaanites: The Duty of Mortification

The Apostle Paul wrote, "For if ye live after the flesh, ye shall die: but if ye through the Spirit do mortify the deeds of the body, ye shall live" (Romans 8:13). In this process of sanctification in the believer, mortifying sin is indispensable. The word *mortify* is the Greek word that means "to put to death, to kill."[107] The English word *mortification* comes from the Latin *mors* (death) and *facere* (to do).[108] Most of what I have learned about the concept of mortification is influenced by *The Mortification of Sin: A Puritan's View of How to Deal with Sin in Your Life* by John Owen, along with his other works.

Mortification has to do with putting something to death. Literally, it means "to make dead."[109] Paul was writing specifically about putting sin to death in the process of our sanctification. There can be no peace treaties with sin in our lives. Paul was calling upon believers to deal thoroughly with sin so that it wouldn't deal thoroughly with them.

Let's be clear, however, that Paul wasn't referring to the final elimination of sin in this life. The believer won't finally be rid of sin until the last stage of salvation, glorification, is complete. Perfection is not possible in this life. Even Paul admitted, "Not as though I had already attained, either were already perfect…" (Philippians 3:12).

In the doctrine of sanctification, there are some who contend that perfection is possible. Certain perfectionist movements have sprung up throughout the history of the church, causing confusion and disillusionment. The Bible clearly teaches that Christians cannot attain sinless perfection in this life. Proverbs 20:9 poses the question: "Who can say, I have made my heart clean, I am pure from my sin?" None of us can. In his masterful work against perfectionism, B. B. Warfield characterized perfectionists as "impatient souls" who "tolerate more readily the idea of an imperfect perfection than the admission of lagging perfecting. They must at all costs have all that is coming to them at once."[110] In other words, perfectionists reject the idea that sanctification is a lifelong process. They insist that it's something God does all at once. Ultimately, however, they must secretly concede, due to experience, that complete Christ-likeness is not possible or redefine sin as something other than what it is. When perfectionists fail, they simply pretend they have no sin. It only makes them more cunning, not more holy.

Mortification is not hiding sin or covering it up. Most people are good at hiding their sins. Many are like Achan. They take the accursed thing and bury it, hoping no one else will know (Joshua 7). What Achan forgot is that you can't hide anything from God. Proverbs 28:13 says, "He that covereth his sins shall not prosper: but whoso confesseth and forsaketh them shall have mercy."

Mortification is not occasional conquests. There are cycles of sin when a certain sin may invade, and you react fervently and express godly sorrow (2 Corinthians 7:11), but sin has a way of lying low and waiting for an opportunity to strike. John Owen wrote, "Yet lust is like a thief that has only lain low in order to start its felony once more."[111] Sin is like the warrior tribe of Amalek. You can think you have beaten it, but it comes back stronger. You can think it's finally gone, and suddenly it will reappear, hitting you at your weakest moment.

Mortification is also not substituting one sin for another. Some Christians struggle with one sin, and in trying to get victory over it, substitute a "smaller" or "more respectable" sin in its place. They exchange the devil for a witch, so to speak. What good is it to trade sins, to trade the lust of the flesh for the lust of the eyes? When this happens, your heart is in danger of being hardened by the deceitfulness of sin. When people are willing to barter sins, it reveals that their motive for getting rid of a particular sin is their own convenience, rather than knowing that it grieves a holy God.

What is mortification? According to John Owen, it's "the habitual weakening of sin."[112] When Paul used the Greek verb *thanatoúte*, "to mortify," in this context, he meant to subdue evil desires springing from our bodily desires.[113] Paul pointed out in Romans 8:12 that believers have no obligation to the body. Here Paul equated "the deeds of the body" (Romans 8:13), meaning the physical body, with the flesh, meaning indwelling sin. Why? Because one's physical body is the means or instrument through which the sin nature operates. In this sense, they are the same.

Mortification is putting to death the deeds of the body, which means subduing or weakening the desires of the flesh. The true believer doesn't live according to the flesh, but according to the Spirit. He or she overcomes and subdues the evil deeds of the body. Paul was describing a pattern of life in which the believer continually seeks to deprive sin of its evil influence.

Paul also called this having "crucified the flesh with the affections and lusts" (Galatians 5:24). John Owen compared the process of mortification to the weakening of a crucified man. He wrote:[114]

> As a man nailed to the cross first struggles and strives, and cries out with great strength and might, but as his blood and spirit waste, his strivings are but faint and seldom, his cries low and hoarse, scarce to be heard: so when a man first sets on a lust or distemper to deal with it, it struggles with great violence to break loose, it cries with earnestness and impatience to be satisfied and relieved; but when, by mortification, the blood and spirits are let out, it moves seldom and faintly, cries sparingly, and is scarce heard in the heart: it may have sometimes a dying pang, that makes an appearance of great vigour and strength, but it is quickly over....

We don't measure our progress in mortification by our restraining of sin, but by how it's progressively weakening within us.

Mortification is a constant watch against sin and a constant war. Joshua went into the land of Canaan and crushed the major military strongholds. He defeated them and won the war, but it was up to the children of Israel to do the mopping up, to clean out the Canaanites afterward. Thus, they were constantly at war with the enemies of God.

Christ won the war against sin, but we must constantly be in warfare in an operation called sanctification. We have to mop up the remaining enemies. We must rid our souls of the Canaanites hiding within. When the Canaanites are no longer a threat, we are mortifying them. For the successful tribes, the Canaanites were weakened and driven out of the cities, and the tribes occupied the cities.

Killing Canaanites:
The Discipline of Mortification

In order to get rid of the Canaanites in our lives that keep us from our spiritual inheritance, we can't afford to have the nonchalant attitude of the children of Manasseh. We must lay aside our pride, presumption, and procrastination. We have to develop a warrior mentality and practice mortification in the following ways.

Daily

The word for *mortify* in Romans 8:13 is a present-tense verb, meaning continual action.[115] Mortification is something that must be done constantly, continually, daily. Victory today doesn't guarantee victory tomorrow. Each new day means there are new Canaanites to put to death.

Romans 8:16 says that we have been adopted into the family of God. In order to enjoy the fellowship of that privilege to the fullest, we must mortify sin daily. Owen wrote:[116]

> But in the ordinary course of daily life, this standing is actualized in the deeds of mortification. Mortification robs sin of its debilitating, inharmonious, and emotionally distracting influences. Without mortification, sin darkens the mind, while the lust of the flesh grows like weeds. Mortification is the soul's vigorous opposition to the fruitless self-life.

Diligently

We can't afford to be passive. We must be proactive. The verb *mortify* in Colossians 3:5 is in the imperative mood, meaning it's a command.[117] In the case of the children of Manasseh, God wasn't making a suggestion when He told them to drive out the Canaanites. Similarly, when God tells the believer today to mortify sin, He is giving an explicit command. We must get serious about this!

We need to be diligent because of the serious nature of sin. We need to be diligent because of sin's power, its strength, and its force. Sin exerts strong influence on our will, on our emotions, and on our minds. It rarely suggests things to us; it almost always makes demands. It rarely leads; it almost always pushes from the rear with driving force. Galatians 5:17 says, "For the flesh lusteth against the Spirit, and the Spirit against the flesh: and these are contrary the one to the other: so that ye cannot do the things that ye would."

Sin finds a willing ally in your flesh (your body) because your flesh is fallen and has a propensity to sin. Because of the depraved Adamic nature, sin springs up constantly within us. It weaves itself into the fabric of our entire being. Even our best deeds are mixed with sin. It's tangled up in our lives.

Decisively

The children of Manasseh made a huge mistake in procrastinating and being indecisive with the Canaanites in their lot. This led to their toleration and, in time, full acceptance of the Canaanites. When it comes to sin, many believers are making the same foolish mistake. In order to have victory and claim what is yours, you must be decisive. Make a solemn vow to oppose all sin in your life, as the psalmist did when he said, "I have sworn, and I will perform it, that I will keep thy righteous judgments" (Psalm 119:106). Be like Daniel, who "purposed in his heart that he would not defile himself" (Daniel 1:8).

Defiantly

As I read Romans 8:12–13, I pick up a defiant tone in the Apostle Paul as he battled sin. Unless you have that kind of defiant determination against sin and for obedience, you will find that you are easily entangled with sin. Bold affirmation and an earnest heart are at the root of all holy living. Until you develop a defiant hatred of sin and genuine love for and commitment to the Lord, you are going to battle the same things over and over—and be defeated. That kind of spirit is expressed by the psalmist in Psalm 119:32: "I will run the way of thy commandments, when thou shalt enlarge my heart."

Secretariat is considered by many experts to be the greatest racehorse in history. The records he set when winning the Triple Crown have never been broken. He won the Belmont Stakes in 1972 by 31 lengths! When the great racehorse finally died, an autopsy was done. They found that this horse was truly a freak of nature! In *Pure Heart*, originally published in the June 4, 1990, issue of *Sports Illustrated*, Bill Nack reported the words of Dr.

Thomas Swerczek, who performed the necropsy that discovered just how big Secretariat's heart was:[118]

> "We were all shocked," Swerczek said. "I've seen and done thousands of autopsies on horses, and nothing I'd ever seen compared to it. The heart of the average horse weighs about nine pounds. This was almost twice the average size, and a third larger than any equine heart I'd ever seen. And it wasn't pathologically enlarged. All the chambers and the valves were normal. It was just larger. I think it told us why he was able to do what he did."

This explains why Secretariat was able to run farther and faster than any other horse in history. His heart was twice the size of a normal horse's! If you, like David, will defiantly make a commitment to lay aside sin, God will equip you spiritually with a heart that's fit to run the race and fight the battles that lie ahead.

Using the Right Weapons

What are the tools or instruments God uses to accomplish this in our lives? There are three: the Holy Spirit, the Word of God, and Christ.

A Person to Love: Christ

Sin is mortified as we focus on Christ, as we focus on the cross and the work accomplished at Calvary. By the way, that's why the Lord's Supper is so meaningful. We contemplate the agony Christ suffered for our sin. This worship experience places in the heart of the believer a holy resolve against sin. John Owen wrote: "...focus your expectations of Christ upon the reality of His death and resurrection.... Act then in faith on the death of Christ expecting it's power in your life; conform to it in your spirit."[119]

It's a spiritual principle that you become like the thing you worship. Psalm 135:15–18 says, "The idols of the heathen are silver and gold, the work of men's hands. They have mouths, but they speak not; eyes have they, but they see not; They have ears, but they hear not; neither is there any breath in their mouths. *They that make them are like unto them*: so is every one that trusteth in them" (emphasis added). If the heathen become like the lifeless gods they worship, how much more will Christians become like Christ since they have the Holy Spirit working to accomplish that very goal?

Paul wrote, "But we all, with open face beholding as in a glass the glory of the Lord, are changed into the same image from glory to glory, even as by the Spirit of the Lord" (2 Corinthians 3:18). As we, through the pages of Scripture, see the glory of Christ and focus on that glory, we are not only empowered, but lifted to new levels of sanctification and victory.

Another way to focus on the glory of Christ is to commune with Him in prayer. True prayer gives the heart a sense of its own vile character and renews the hatred of sin. Owen wrote, "He who pleads with God for the remission of sin also pleads with his own heart to detest it."[120] Somewhere along the line in your prayer life, you need to get honest and say to God, "I want You to reveal my sin. Shine the spotlight of Your holiness into my dark heart and show me the real state of my heart." Pray, like the psalmist, "Search me, O God, and know my heart: try me, and know my thoughts: And see if there be any wicked way in me, and lead me in the way everlasting" (Psalm 139:23–24).

A Power to Live: The Spirit

Romans 8:13 says that mortification takes place through the Holy Spirit. He convicts us of sins. When we are yielded to Him, we won't seek to satisfy the flesh:

> *This I say then, Walk in the Spirit, and ye shall not fulfil the lust of the flesh.*
> **—Galatians 5:16**

If you want to have victory in your life, simply walk in the Spirit. You will find that the Holy Spirit of God will lift you up to have victory over any sin in your life. Some preachers say, "If you quit doing this and quit doing that, then you'll have the fullness of the power of the Holy Spirit." If I could quit doing those things, I wouldn't need the Holy Spirit. I can't quit doing those things. It's the Holy Spirit who gives me the power to rise above sin in my life. As evangelist Roy Hession wrote, "The Holy Spirit is not the reward of your faithfulness, but God's gift for your weakness...."[121]

We must consciously yield to the Holy Spirit and actively depend on Him. We also need to understand that the Holy Spirit sometimes works monergistically—that is, He sometimes works alone, without our conscious involvement. The benediction in Hebrews 13:20–21 speaks of God "working in you that which is wellpleasing in his sight." That should encourage us! Even in those defeated and dismal days when we see little progress in the battle against sin, we can be confident that the Holy Spirit is still at work in us.

John Owen listed several things the Holy Spirit does in this process of mortification:[122]

> (1) He convinces the heart clearly and fully of evil and guilt that needs to be mortified.
>
> (2) He reveals the fullness of Christ for our relief.
>
> (3) He establishes the heart's expectation of help from Christ.
>
> (4) He brings the cross of Christ to our hearts with its sin killing power.
>
> (5) He is the author and finisher of our sanctification.
>
> (6) He helps us as we pray.

Principles to Learn: The Word of God

In this process of putting sin to death, there's no substitute for knowing God's Word. Earlier in the book of Joshua, we saw a threefold command that God gave to Joshua and Israel concerning the Word of God: "This book of the law shall not depart out of thy mouth; but thou shalt meditate therein day and night, that thou mayest observe to do according to all that is written therein" (Joshua

1:8). God was saying, "Don't stop talking about it and meditating on it. The result will be a change in your actions."

This is a little formula I like to refer to as "memorization, meditation, modification." You begin to do the things you think about. If you are constantly meditating on Scripture, you will begin to act accordingly. It's simple but profound. Scripture also has life-giving power. It strengthens us to do what we ought to do. When a heart is controlled by the Word of God, saying no to sin is easy. If you memorize and meditate, your life will be modified, and sin will be mortified. You will be able to face your enemies.

Conquering Your Inheritance

We have been on a great adventure with Joshua—crossing swollen rivers, scaling large city walls, pursuing the enemy, driving out Canaanites, defeating giants, possessing the inheritance, and always calling upon God for miraculous intervention. Joshua is the Old Testament book that illustrates New Testament victory.

For whatsoever is born of God overcometh the world: and this is the victory that overcometh the world, even our faith.
—1 John 5:4

You can apply the same principle to yourself spiritually. Just as Joshua and Israel had a Canaan to conquer, Christians have an inheritance that we must claim: victory over sin, death, and the devil. What a shame it would be to study this book and still not experience the victory God wants you to have!

What was a military reality for the children of Israel is a spiritual reality for you. Jesus won the victory for you on Calvary. He won a major battle, defeating the evil kings of sin and Satan and death. Now it's up to you to claim the victory, to live in that victory, and to walk in that victory.

WORKBOOK

Chapter Ten Questions

Question: What are some sins that you think of as harmless or minor? What is keeping you from driving them out of your life? How does each of them have the potential to grow into a destructive force in your life and in the body of Christ?

_____

_____

_____

_____

_____

_____

_____

_____

_____

Question: What is your attitude toward sin? Is your treatment of sin nonchalant, or do you view it as something that needs to be utterly mortified? Look at the characteristics needed for mastering the discipline of mortification daily, diligently, decisively, and defiantly. Do those descriptions categorize your endeavors to mortify sin in your life? How can Christ, the Spirit, and the Word of God help you in this process of mortification?

_____

_____

_____

_____

_____

_____

_____

_____

_____

_____

Journal: What are the areas where you are reaching your potential in Christ? Where are you falling short? Imagine and journal about what your life would be if you were the person you can be for good and for God. (Keep in mind that this has more to do with *who you are* than *what you do* and that the process of sanctification will continue from salvation until you reach heaven.)

_____

_____

_____

_____

_____

_____

_____

_____

_____

_____

_____

Action: Read Romans 6–8 and Galatians 5. Write your own working definition of what it means to walk in the Spirit.

Chapter Ten Notes

CHAPTER ELEVEN

Christ, Our Refuge
Joshua 20:1–9

Big Idea: The cities of refuge beautifully portray the refuge people can find when they run to Christ.

Undoubtedly, one of the greatest hymn writers of the church was Charles Wesley. Many, myself included, believe that the hymn "Jesus, Lover of My Soul" was his masterpiece. The great American preacher Henry Ward Beecher eloquently stated:[123]

> I would rather have written that hymn of Wesley's ... than to have the fame of all the kings that ever sat on earth. It is more glorious. It has more power in it. ... But that hymn will go on singing until the last trump brings forth the angel band; and then, I think, it will mount up on some lip to the very presence of God.

There's a wonderful story told about the writing of this hymn:[124]

> Mr. Wesley was standing before the open window of his room one morning. He was looking out over the beautiful landscape which was in front of his home. As he looked he saw a little song bird which was being chased by a cruel hawk. The poor bird was badly frightened, and seeing an open window, flew through it and directly into Mr. Wesley's arms. With fluttering heart and quivering wing it nestled close to the singer and escaped a cruel death in the talons of the hawk. According to the story, Mr. Wesley himself was just then having some personal trials and was feeling the need of a refuge just as the little bird, which had flown into his bosom for protection. Out of this incident and his personal experience, he took up his pen and produced the masterpiece of his many hymns....

Jesus, lover of my soul,
Let me to Thy bosom fly,
While the nearer waters roll,
While the tempest still is high!
Hide me, O my Savior, hide,
Till the storm of life is past;
Safe into the haven guide;
O receive my soul at last!

The words reflect a deep desire in us to find refuge from the burdens and trials of this life. Since Adam's fall and expulsion from the Garden of Eden, mankind has been running and seeking a refuge. This world and all that is in it offers no real haven. The refuge it offers is weak and insufficient to meet man's deepest need. God has designed it that way so man may learn that his only true refuge is in God. The psalmist knew this and wrote:

I looked on my right hand, and beheld, but there was no man that would know me: refuge failed me; no man cared for my soul. I cried unto thee, O Lord: I said, Thou art my refuge and my portion in the land of the living.
—Psalm 142:4–5

This is the lesson we take from Joshua 20. This chapter, to me, presents one of the most beautiful portraits of salvation in all of the Old Testament. It portrays the unshakable refuge a person finds when he or she runs to Christ.

Seeing Christ in the Old Testament

There are two ways we can read the Bible. One way is man-centered. People can read the Bible thinking that it's basically about them and what they must do to be right with God. The second way is Christ-centered. This approach views everything as about Christ and what He has done to make us absolutely right with God. This is the right way to read the Bible, the way Christ would have us read it.

It's as if Jesus Christ is saying, "If you can't see Me, you won't be able to read the Bible correctly. You won't be able to understand salvation by grace, through faith, without works. You'll never have that sure refuge and hope." Once we understand that it's all about Christ, we know true peace, have our future guaranteed, and can face anything.

Do you remember the story of Jesus on the road to Emmaus after His resurrection? Luke 24 records when Jesus met two disciples on that road. He gave them a gentle rebuke for their ignorance of the Old Testament Scriptures. Then, "beginning at Moses and all the prophets, he expounded unto them in all the scriptures the things concerning himself" (Luke 24:27).

What an exposition of Scripture that must have been! I would give all my years of college and seminary education just to have been in that Bible study when the living Word taught the written Word. Jesus went through the entire Old Testament, showing how it pointed to Him. Earlier Jesus had challenged the unbelieving Jews, saying:

> *Search the scriptures; for in them ye think ye have eternal life: and they are they which testify of me.*
> **—John 5:39**

When it comes to interpreting and understanding Scripture, one great principle that must guide us is what the reformers and church theologians call Christocentric hermeneutics. *Hermeneutics* is a word that describes the principles of interpretation. The central question in Christocentric interpretation is: "What does this passage say about Christ?" or "How does this passage point to Christ?" While the reformers rejected allegorical interpretation (the idea that there's some secret spiritual meaning below the surface of the literal meaning), they nevertheless relied on typology and other creative hermeneutical strategies to discern how Christ was the subject matter of the Old Testament.

It was the great reformer Martin Luther, above all, who made this Christocentric principle famous. He said, "The entire Old Testament refers to Christ."[125] He also stated that "the Old Testament is the epistle of Christ, which after His death He opened and caused to be read through the Gospel and proclaimed everywhere."[126] Luther likened Scripture to the cloth in which the baby Jesus was wrapped. He stated that the "law and the prophets are not rightly preached or known save we see Christ wrapped up in them."[127]

Luther would say to us that when we read the book of Joshua, we should look for Christ. He may not be in every verse, but He is certainly somewhere in every chapter or on every page. Through Christocentric eyes, we can see Christ in Joshua 20 in the cities of refuge, which point to our real refuge in Christ.

Appoint Cities of Refuge

The book of Joshua can be divided into two main parts: chapters 1–12, which describe the conquest of Canaan, and chapters 13–24, which describe the division of the land. One can get the impression that the conquest of the land was accomplished very quickly. While it's true that major decisive victories were won in a matter of months, the wars that brought defeat to the major cities and strongholds took approximately seven years.[128]

Soon after the conquest stage, Joshua, who was very old by that time, began to assign land to the various tribes.

Israel's camp was moved from Gilgal to Shiloh, which was in the high country between Ai and Gerizim. Chapters 13–19 detail the location of land inherited by each tribe. Part of the process included casting lots to determine the matter (Joshua 18:6). Chapters 20–21 list two groups of special cities that served a unique purpose. Chapter 21 lists forty-eight cities of the Levites, who were priests. Chapter 20 focuses on six cities that were appointed as "cities of refuge," taken from among the forty-eight cities of the Levites. The cities of refuge were established by the direct command of God as a way to promote a universal code of justice, as we will see.

We all know that accidents happen. Sometimes someone even dies because of a mistake. Joshua, by command of God, named a city of refuge in six strategic territories. These cities were places where an accused person could go to seek sanctuary and justice. God wanted people to have a safe shelter to run to when they needed a refuge.

As you study the names and purpose of these cities, you will again see how the Old Testament anticipates the New Testament, where Jesus Himself became our refuge. Three things in the book of Joshua illustrate the refuge we have in Jesus Christ:

- the purpose of the cities of refuge
- the portrait of the cities
- the placement of the cities.

The Purpose of the Cities

A city of refuge was a place to flee in case of an incident in which someone's life was accidentally taken. These cities protected the accused from being killed by a relative of the victim until the accused could be tried in court:

> The LORD also spake unto Joshua, saying, Speak to the children of Israel, saying, Appoint out for you cities of refuge, whereof I spake unto you by the hand of Moses: That the slayer that killeth any person unawares and unwittingly may flee thither: and they shall be your refuge from the avenger of blood.
> —Joshua 20:1–3

If a person was involved in an accident that killed another person, perhaps while working or in some bizarre misfortune, a city of refuge would provide a place to flee until the matter could be heard legally.

In that ancient Near Eastern society, when a family member was killed, either intentionally or unintentionally, another family member would be appointed as the avenger of blood. It was the duty of the avenger to track down and kill the murderer. Donald Campbell wrote, "In the ancient world, blood revenge was widely practiced. When a person was killed, his nearest relative took responsibility for vengeance." This was called a *vendetta,* and often "vendettas were handed down from generation to generation."[129]

This ancient system of justice was fine for

premeditated murder, but what if the killing was unintentional? After all, tragic accidents do take place. A person may be responsible for some form of negligence, but God's law didn't punish accidental killing with death. It would be wrong if the avenger were allowed to proceed.[130] There were no advanced court systems in the ancient world like we have today. When someone had a vendetta against him, he would become a fugitive because of the immediate danger and would need to flee to a place of refuge.

God made it clear that the murder had to be unintentional. This was not an arrangement for a murderer seeking to avoid justice, but for a person whose crime was manslaughter. In our courts today, there's a clear distinction between first-degree murder and manslaughter. According to legal experts, manslaughter is:[131]

> ...an unlawful killing that doesn't involve malice aforethought—intent to seriously harm or kill, or extreme, reckless disregard for life. The absence of malice aforethought means that manslaughter involves less moral blame than either first or second degree murder. Thus, while manslaughter is a serious crime, the punishment for it is generally less than that for murder. The two main variations of manslaughter are usually referred to as voluntary and involuntary manslaughter. Voluntary manslaughter is often called a "heat of passion" crime. It occurs when a person is strongly provoked (under circumstances that could similarly provoke a reasonable person) and kills in the heat of passion aroused by that provocation. Involuntary manslaughter often refers to unintentional homicide from criminally negligent or reckless conduct. It can also refer to an unintentional killing through commission of a crime other than a felony.

By using the words "unawares" and "unwittingly" (Joshua 20:3), "without enmity" (Numbers 35:22), and "ignorantly" (Deuteronomy 19:4), Scripture makes it clear that this is what our legal system today would call *involuntary manslaughter*.

Deuteronomy 19 gives an example. Two men were chopping wood. One man's axe head wasn't very well attached to the handle. While he was chopping wood, the axe head accidently flew off and killed the other man. Obviously, this was a terrible accident. Should the man have been more responsible about checking his axe to make sure that the head was securely fastened? Yes! Was this unintentional and without malice? Of course. The narrative says that the man "shall flee unto one of those cities, and live: Lest the avenger of the blood pursue the slayer, while his heart is hot, and overtake him … and slay him; whereas he was not worthy of death, inasmuch as he hated him not in time past" (Deuteronomy 19:5–6).

Once he reached the city, the terrified fugitive would appear before judges at the city gate and declare his case before them. If they found the story to be legitimate, that the death happened without malice or forethought and was indeed accidental, the fugitive would be allowed to enter the city. He would remain there, if necessary, until the death of the high priest serving at that time.

These cities of refuge speak prophetically and typically of Christ. The writer of Hebrews probably had these cities in mind when he wrote:

That by two immutable things, in which it was impossible for God to lie, we might have a strong consolation, who have fled for refuge to lay hold upon the hope set before us....

—Hebrews 6:18

He was writing about the refuge and hope we have in Jesus Christ! Did you know that every one of us is a fugitive running from the consequence of sin? Just as a guilty man fled to a city of refuge for protection and asylum, you and I need to flee to Christ for refuge. Why? Because we are guilty of a death. Whose death? The death of Christ! I am guilty of a death because it was my sin that put Christ on the cross. Ask yourself, "Who is responsible for the death of Jesus?" Was it the Jews who said, "Crucify him"? Was it the Romans, who nailed Him to the cross? All of them do bear some culpability. Ultimately, however, it was my sin and your sin—the sin of every human being—that put Jesus on the cross.

I am guilty of the death and the murder of Jesus Christ, and so are you. You may argue, "Now, wait a minute! We didn't know. We didn't mean for our sins to cause His death!" Yes, I know. We didn't do it with malice, but ignorantly. We did it unawares, unwittingly, and without enmity, but it was our sin just the same. Remember what Jesus said on the cross: "Father, forgive them; for they know not what they do" (Luke 23:34). He died for your sins and mine.

The Portrait of the Cities

And they appointed Kedesh in Galilee in mount Naphtali, and Shechem in mount Ephraim, and Kirjatharba, which is

Hebron, in the mountain of Judah. And on the other side Jordan by Jericho eastward, they assigned Bezer in the wilderness upon the plain out of the tribe of Reuben, and Ramoth in Gilead out of the tribe of Gad, and Golan in Bashan out of the tribe of Manasseh.

—Joshua 20:7–8

Certain cities in the Bible have names with a definite significance. For example, in Joshua 15 when Caleb conquered Kadesh-arba (meaning "city of Arba"), he renamed it Hebron for a purpose. Hebron is one of the cities of refuge. Many cities in Scripture are named to convey some idea or characteristic about it. Jacob named a place Bethel ("house of God") right after he had a vision of a stairway coming from heaven to the place where he lay that night (Genesis 28:19).

Scripture gives other examples like that for city names. The great expositor H. A. Ironside was perhaps the first person to see truths that point to Christ in the meanings of the names of these six cities. He wrote, "It would seem as though the names of the six cities of refuge have suggestive meaning: at least they may well bring our minds to some of the privileges that are ours in Christ."[132]

Kadesh is the Hebrew word for "holiness."[133] Holiness speaks to me about Christ, my Savior. The Bible says that without holiness, no one will see God (Hebrews 12:14). No one can get to heaven on his or her own. You cannot be in God's presence without holiness, and you have no holiness of your own. Scripture is clear that all men and women are sinners by birth, by nature, and by practice (Romans 3:10, 23). Since we have no holiness, it must come from another source. When you place your faith in the finished work of Christ, He erases all sin from your record and places on your record all of His holiness (2 Corinthians 5:21). This is called the doctrine of imputation because the holiness or righteousness of Christ is imputed to your account (Romans 4:5–8). You will get to heaven only through the righteousness of Christ.

Shechem, in Mount Ephraim, means "shoulder."[134] This speaks to me about Christ, my strength. A shoulder is where you carry your burdens. Christ is the one who carries my burdens. He is my strength. Do you remember the story of the good shepherd? When he found the lost sheep, he laid it on his shoulders (Luke 15:4–7). In Exodus, the high priest wore a robe with two gold plates, one on each shoulder. On the gold plates were the names of the twelve tribes of Israel, six on one and six on the other. It was a picture of how God carries His people. His strength and His shoulders carry us. Isaiah 9:6 says that "the government shall be upon his shoulder." Thank God that He carries us and our burdens!

Hebron means "fellowship" or "fullness."[135] This speaks to me about Christ, my satisfaction. One of the greatest blessings of salvation is fellowship with Jesus Christ. We were created to have fellowship with God, and people try to fill that void with the world and earthly things.

Bezer means "stronghold" or "fortification." [136] This speaks of Christ, my security. The Bible says, "The name of the LORD is a strong tower: the righteous runneth into it, and is safe" (Proverbs 18:10). I don't need to fear anything if Christ is my security.

Ramoth means "high place exalted."[137] That speaks to me of Christ, my sovereign. Sometimes I hear people say, "I accept Jesus as my Savior, but not as my Lord." That's impossible. There's no such dichotomy in Scripture.

> *That if thou shalt confess with thy mouth the Lord Jesus, and shalt believe in thine heart that God hath raised him from the dead, thou shalt be saved. For with the heart man believeth unto righteousness; and with the mouth confession is made unto salvation.*
> **—Romans 10:9–10**

When I got saved, Jesus took me as I was, a guilty sinner, and I took Jesus as He is, the *Lord* Jesus Christ.

Golan, in Bashan out of the tribe of Manasseh, means "separation."[138][139] This speaks to me of Christ, my sanctification. Sanctification is the process by which God is making you more like Christ and less like the world. You have a desire to walk away from the things of this world, say no to sin, and say yes to Christ and righteousness.

Christ is my savior, my strength, my satisfaction, my security, my sovereign, and my sanctification. The names of these cities teach us that Christ is all we need!

The Placement of the Cities

The Holy Land is about the size of the state of Maryland, where I was born and raised. Just like the state of Maryland is divided in the middle by the Chesapeake Bay, forming an eastern shore and a western side, the promised land was divided by the Jordan River, with tribes living on both sides. There were three cities of refuge on the west side of the Jordan—Kadesh, Shechem, and Hebron—and three cities on the east side—Golan, Ramoth, and Bezer. These cities were so located and designated by Almighty God that no matter where you were in the promised land, you were always close to a city of refuge.

Roads were never clogged to these cities. According to Levitical law, the roads had to be kept in good shape. James Montgomery Boice pointed out that "bridges were built over ravines, so the fugitive could take the shortest route possible."[140] The priests had the duty of making sure that the roads leading to these cities were clear of any obstruction. One day a year, during the springtime, people were sent to repair the roads. This reminds us of our duty. As believers in Christ, we are now priests of God (1 Peter 2:5). We are to keep the way to Christ clear! How can sinners find their way to Christ unless we help them? We must build bridges and keep the roads to Christ in excellent shape.

The gates were never closed. In ancient days, every city had a wall around it, and in the front, there was a gate. At nighttime, they would close and lock the gate as a protective measure, but not so for the cities of refuge. No matter what time of day or night it was, the gates on the cities of refuge were never closed. They were open twenty-four hours a day, seven days a week, 365 days a year, every year. This reminds us that the arms of Jesus are always open to any who come to Him. Jesus said, "…him that cometh to me I will in no wise cast out" (John 6:37). If you want refuge, Christ is waiting with open arms!

The direction was never confused. Every crossroad pointed to a city of refuge. They had signs all along the way, all throughout the Holy Land, pointing the direction to these cities. On the signs was the Hebrew word *Miklat*, which means "refuge."[141] No one wanted a fugitive to take the wrong road. In addition, the signs were made so big that any man who was running hard could read them without stopping.[142]

The cities of refuge were not only for Jews; they were open to people of all races. It didn't matter if you were Jew or gentile, rich or poor, slave or free, male or female, educated or uneducated. The cities of refuge were available for all. This reminds us of the wonderful way of salvation, which is available to all. If the manslayer didn't want to go to a city of refuge, there was no other provision in the law for him. In other words, outside of the city of refuge, there was no hope.

Think about your access to Christ in this light. The road leading to Him is always clear. On His side, there are no obstructions. When He died on the cross, He died for all sin, so sin is not a problem that can keep you from coming.

He cleared the way! The only things that can keep you from getting to Him are unbelief and pride.

If you want mercy, you will find it if you come to Jesus. The way to Him is clearly marked. God placed the sign-post we call the Bible. It's clear in what it teaches you about Jesus Christ. It tells you that He is the only way to God. No matter who you are, no matter where you are, no matter what time of day or night it is, He is always available.

You are being pursued by an avenger called death. He is relentless in his pursuit. You may live a long time, but eventually death will catch you. Who knows when he will appear? It could be this year, this month, this hour! Your only hope is to flee to Christ, who is "the resurrection, and the life" (John 11:25). Whoever believes in Him will have eternal life (John 3:16).

There's a story in 2 Samuel 3 relating a time when someone died needlessly instead of seeking refuge. Abner was a mighty warrior and a good man, and David genuinely mourned over him: "And the king lamented over Abner, and said, Died Abner as a fool dieth?" (2 Samuel 3:33).

Why did David say this? Abner died needlessly because he left a city of refuge to talk with his enemy. As with most military conflicts, the details are complex. Abner was abandoning a skirmish with David's troops when Joab's younger brother, Asahel, pursued him. Abner tried to convince Asahel to stop and to fight someone else, but Asahel persisted and charged at Abner. Abner was the stronger fighter. He didn't want to kill Asahel, but he did. It was self-defense. He had no choice (2 Samuel 2:12–32).

Abner returned to Hebron, a city of refuge, but Joab, as Asahel's older brother, was now Asahel's avenger of blood. He hated Abner and wanted vengeance. Abner was at the gate of a city of refuge. All he had to do was go inside the gate and he would have been safe, but instead he walked into Joab's trap. Then Joab killed him (2 Samuel 3:26–30). Abner died needlessly, as a fool dies, walking away from his refuge. David lamented, "Thy hands were not bound, nor thy feet put into fetters: as a man falleth before wicked men, so fellest thou" (2 Samuel 3:34). No one forced Abner to do what he did. He was free to make his own decision about claiming refuge.

Consider the final stanzas of Charles Wesley's grand hymn and allow it to remind you of your only real refuge:[143]

Thou, O Christ, art all I want,
More than all in Thee I find;
Raise the fallen, cheer the faint,
Heal the sick, and lead the blind.

Just and holy is Thy name,
I am all unrighteousness;
False and full of sin I am;
Thou art full of truth and grace.

Plenteous grace with Thee is found,
Grace to cover all my sin;
Let the healing streams abound;
Make and keep me pure within.

Thou of life the fountain art,
Freely let me take of Thee;
Spring Thou up within my heart;
Rise to all eternity.

God has given you free will to make your own decisions. You may be at the very gate of salvation, on the brink of placing your life in Christ as your refuge. But the avenger of blood, Satan, speaks enticing words to you. He lies. He wants to pull you away—through circumstances, through material things, through feelings—from the only safe place there is: life with Jesus Christ. The smartest thing you can do is enter that refuge and then encourage others to do the same!

WORKBOOK

Chapter Eleven Questions

Question: How are the names of the cities of refuge an illustration of Christ? What can you learn about salvation from God's instructions about the cities of refuge?

_____

_____

_____

_____

_____

_____

_____

_____

_____

_____

_____

Question: What are some things that you have allowed to clog the road between you and Christ? How can you clear the way to restore fellowship with Him?

_____

_____

_____

_____

_____

_____

_____

_____

_____

_____

_____

Journal: Who is an "Abner" in your life—someone who knows the way to forgiveness, safety, and salvation in Christ but is wavering just outside the gate? Write down your prayer for this person and ask God for an opportunity to speak with him or her about the need for Christ.

_____

_____

_____

_____

_____

_____

_____

_____

_____

_____

_____

_____

Action: Choose one of the cities of refuge and do a Scripture study to see what other noteworthy events happened there. How does knowing that city was a city of refuge give perspective on its history?

Chapter Eleven Notes

CHAPTER TWELVE

The Last Words of a Faithful Old Soldier
Joshua 23:1–24:33

Big Idea: *Believers will never be able to enjoy the full blessings of their spiritual inheritance if they become complacent.*

April 19, 1951

The world has turned over many times since I took the oath on the plain at West Point, and the hopes and dreams have long since vanished, but I still remember the refrain of one of the most popular barrack ballads of that day which proclaimed proudly that 'old soldiers never die; they just fade away.' And like that old soldier in that ballad, I now close my military career and just fade away, an old soldier who tried to do his duty as God gave him the sight to see that duty. [144]

—General Douglas MacArthur

1290 B.C.—the book of Joshua ends on a similar note, with an old soldier giving the Israelites his final thoughts before fading into history. Joshua was at the end of his career and would soon die. He was worried. Now that the lives of the Israelites were easier, would they maintain their commitment and dependence on God? Joshua longed to influence them and warn them.

> *And it came to pass a long time after that the LORD had given rest unto Israel from all their enemies round about, that Joshua waxed old and stricken in age.*
> *—Joshua 23:1*

Chapter 23 records that Joshua first met with all the leaders of Israel. Then, in chapter 24, he met with all the people. He knew that the people had seen the mighty works of God, but now that they were settled in the land, the power and the glory of God would diminish in their daily routine. He knew that the old guard, those who knew Moses and Joshua, were swiftly dying off. A new generation was coming to the forefront. Before he died, Joshua wanted to remind all of Israel, young and old, about their unique covenant with God and the disaster that would befall them if they worshiped other gods.

We also live in an age when many have forgotten about the glory and the power of God. A comfortable and prosperous lifestyle can make God seem irrelevant. Future generations could abandon God altogether unless you pass on your faith to your children and their friends. Carefully consider Joshua's last words to his people and take them to heart.

Joshua's Concerns:
Beware of Complacency!

And Joshua called for all Israel, and for their elders, and for their heads, and for their judges, and for their officers, and said unto them, I am old and stricken in age: And ye have seen all that the LORD your God hath done unto all these nations because of you; for the LORD your God is he that hath fought for you.
— Joshua 23:2–3

The scene of this speech to the elders and Israel was no doubt Shiloh, where the tabernacle was located at that time. It was the center of the land possessed by the tribe of Ephraim. Ephraim was Joshua's tribe. Therefore, making Shiloh the spiritual and political capital of Israel at that time made good sense. Before there was the temple in Jerusalem, there was the tabernacle in Shiloh.

I have had the privilege of doing archaeological digs at Shiloh. Evidence points to the fact that the tabernacle, for a time, may have been placed on a hill at that location. When I picture this scene in my mind, I fancy Joshua standing just outside the gate of the tabernacle on a hill, with the elders and children of Israel just below. It would have been a place where he could have been easily heard.

Joshua proceeded to give them his "old soldier" speech. You can read between the lines that Joshua had some real concerns. He felt compelled to address these urgent issues while he was still alive. I love what Joshua said, how he reminded them, "Look, it wasn't me who drove out anyone. It was the Lord who did it all."

Their Complacency

Joshua reminded them repeatedly of the faithfulness of God. They needed to continue to obey the Word of God and keep His law. Joshua was afraid they might start taking God's favor for granted. Obedience was the key to continued victory in the land of Canaan. As long as they were obedient to God, He would give them the victory. When they stopped obeying the Lord, their problems began. This is a word for all of us. You can't afford to become complacent when it comes to the Scripture and loving God through your obedience.

In the book of Revelation, Jesus chastised the church at Laodicea:

> *Because thou sayest, I am rich, and increased with goods, and have need of nothing; and knowest not that thou art wretched, and miserable, and poor, and blind, and naked....*
> —**Revelation 3:17**

The church there was no longer pursuing the Lord. Some were self-satisfied with their spiritual condition and, as a result, failed to challenge things in their lives that led them away from God and deeper into sin. This is a description of many people and churches today.

Their Compromise

Joshua also feared Israel's compromise. If the people of Israel abandoned serving the Lord, Yahweh, they would begin to serve the dead gods of Canaan. You must always cleave to the Lord and not have any other gods. A god or an idol is anything that you love, serve, think about, and depend upon more than God. The truth is that our culture is full of idolatry. Sadly, this is even true among Christians in the church. Many are guilty of compromise. Do you indulge in activities that you know God disapproves of? Do you do things that you know are wrong and try to justify it by the fact that you know somebody else who does those things?

Many have compromised their standards and given in to the will of their flesh. Spiritual compromise has been a problem for the church since the very beginning. Don't allow yourself to compromise your Christian life in any way. Remember the Apostle Paul's admonition: "Abstain from all appearance of evil" (1 Thessalonians 5:22).

Their Lack of Commitment

> But cleave unto the LORD your God, as ye have done unto this day.
> —*Joshua 23:8*

Jesus Christ must be number one. This should be the major objective of the church. We want people who are fully committed to Jesus Christ. Everyone around you should be able to see your faith by how you live, not only by what you say. Your children should see it and feel secure in their own faith.

Joshua's Challenge: Remember What God Has Done for You!

Joshua challenged the people to look at what the Lord had done and what the Lord was currently doing. If the Israelites would look at what the Lord was doing each day, then they would more likely serve Him. His love and His care for them would be abundantly apparent.

God's Wrath

To paraphrase Joshua 23:9–13, "If you serve the Lord, He will bless you. He will continue to drive out your enemies, and one of you can chase a thousand if you obey the Lord. If you disobey the Lord, He will chastise you. He will punish you."

This was a perfect indicator of the nation's love for God. If you love the Lord, then obey Him, and He will bless you. As a child of God, you have two possible ways of living your life. You can either live it within the confines of God's will and be blessed, or you can live outside of the will of God and be chastised.

God's Works

The scene moved from Shiloh to a new location. All of Israel assembled again in Shechem. Shechem was holy ground to the Israelites. It was at Shechem that God promised Abraham that his descendants would inherit the land (Genesis 12:6–7). It was also the place where Jacob built an altar (Genesis 33:20). Remember that Shechem was located between Mount Ebal and Mount Gerizim, where the people of Israel had previously affirmed their commitment to the Lord (Joshua 8:30–35). This was probably the same type of assembly as before. There were six tribes on one mountain and six tribes on the other. Joshua addressed the nation again. In the first address, the keywords were *nation* and *land*. Now the keyword is the LORD.

When you read Joshua 24:3–12, two things stand out. First, God is the one doing the talking here. Second, you can't help but notice all the instances of *I*:

- "I took your father Abraham…" (v. 3).
- "I gave unto Isaac…" (v. 4).
- "I sent Moses…" (v. 5).
- "I brought your fathers…" (v. 6).
- "I brought you into the land…" (v. 8).
- "I sent the hornet before you…" (v. 12).
- "I have given you a land…" (v. 13).

Joshua was speaking on behalf of God as a prophet. He said to remember the mighty works of God. That also applies to us today in the church. If you remember what the Lord did and see what God is doing in the present, it will motivate you to serve the Lord as you should.

You must remember Jesus. You must remember what He did. Think of how He loved you when you were lost. Think about how He has forgiven you for all your sins, how He has picked you up when you have failed and has loved you anyway. Think about His greatness and His goodness. Let all His blessings motivate you to serve the Lord with your whole heart!

God's Will

> Now therefore fear the LORD, and serve him in sincerity and in truth: and put away the gods which your fathers served on the other side of the flood, and in Egypt; and serve ye the LORD. And if it seem evil unto you to serve the LORD, choose you this day whom ye will serve; whether the gods which your fathers served that were on the other side of the flood, or the gods of the Amorites, in whose land ye dwell: but as for me and my house, we will serve the LORD.
> **—Joshua 24:14–15**

Joshua made it clear. You are going to serve someone, so be sure you choose who that is. There's no neutral ground. Make a choice. Not choosing is itself a choice.

To serve (*abad*) means to fear God, obey Him, and worship only Him.[145] It means to love Him and fix your heart upon Him, obeying Him because you want to, not because you must. Your service is an act of worship because you are expressing thanks to God for everything He has done for you. Sometimes people go to church and just follow the crowd. Don't do that. Set the standards. That's what Joshua did. His words in Scripture are a clarion call, even today. Many people who read little Scripture can still recite this passage of total commitment from the book of Joshua.

God wants you to search your life and destroy anything in it that hinders your walk with Him. Lose the mindset of looking at others and measuring yourself against how they are doing. Sadly, not everyone serves the Lord with total commitment. Your standard is none other than the Lord Jesus Christ! God saved you to be like Him, and that's what you should desire.

God's Witness

And Joshua said unto the people, Ye cannot serve the LORD: for he is an holy God; he is a jealous God; he will not forgive your transgressions nor your sins.
—Joshua 24:19

Joshua reminded the people of Israel that they could not be halfhearted. If you call yourself a Christian and you live as the world lives, that's taking the Lord's name in vain. Joshua wasn't saying that God is unforgiving, but if they deliberately served idols, there was no forgiveness under the law. Remember that God is your witness and you can't hide sin: "The eyes of the LORD are in every place, beholding the evil and the good" (Proverbs 15:3).

Joshua's Covenant: Renew Your Commitment to the Lord!

So Joshua made a covenant with the people that day, and set them a statute and an ordinance in Shechem. And Joshua wrote these words in the book of the law of God, and took a great stone, and set it up there under an oak, that was by the sanctuary of the LORD. And Joshua said unto all the people, Behold, this stone shall be a witness unto us; for it hath heard all the words of the LORD which he spake unto

> us: it shall be therefore a witness unto you, lest ye deny
> your God.
>
> —*Joshua 24:25–27*

Old Testament scholars agree that the literary form of chapter 24 follows the literary form of ancient treaties between a king and his subjects. It's called a suzerain-vassal treaty form. These treaties entailed a periodic renewal, and accordingly, Joshua 24 is a covenant renewal document. The covenant established at Mount Sinai was not an everlasting covenant; it had to be renewed in every generation. That renewal was now unfolding with a new generation of Israelites. This kind of ritual normally involved stones.[146]

Joshua's last official act as the leader of Israel was to lead this new generation to renew the covenant with the Lord. Whenever the people of Israel would go to Shechem, they could see this gray stone under this tree, and they would be reminded of the covenant relationship they had with Almighty God. They made a promise to be faithful to Him, so this covenant involved a stone of great size. It was a marker. It was a memorial.

I remember when the Lord placed the call on my heart to preach. There was a place in the woods close by my house where I went sometimes to be alone. Finding a quiet spot in my home with three brothers was a challenge, so that certain spot by a specific oak tree became a special place for me. I spent a lot of time reading and praying at that spot. While I was there one day, reading 2 Timothy 4:2–5, God impressed it deeply on me to preach the Word. When I obeyed what I believed to be the call of God and made a commitment to preach the Word, I took a big piece of bark off that tree to remember that commitment. To me, the bark was a spiritual marker and a reminder to keep my commitment. Spiritual memorials and markers are good because they remind us to guard against complacency and to keep our commitments to the Lord.

When you make a decision before God, He expects you to honor it. Are you doing all the things you told the Lord you would do? If not, today would be a good day to make things right with the Lord. We are warned in Scripture that God regards decisions and commitments as serious. You might have forgotten about it, but He hasn't! It's far better never to make a promise to God than to make it and then break it:

> Keep thy foot when thou goest to the house of God, and be more ready to hear, than to give the sacrifice of fools: for they consider not that they do evil. Be not rash with thy mouth, and let not thine heart be hasty to utter any thing before God: for God is in heaven, and thou upon earth: therefore let thy words be few. For a dream cometh through the multitude of business; and a fool's voice is known by multitude of words. When thou vowest a vow unto God, defer not to pay it; for he hath no pleasure in fools: pay that which thou hast vowed. Better is it that thou shouldest not vow, than that thou shouldest vow and not pay.
>
> —*Ecclesiastes 5:1–5*

The Gravestone Memorials

Joshua erected this great stone as a memorial, but the covenant also included some gravestones. The book of

Joshua closes with three funerals and gravestones.

1. The first was that of Joshua.

> *And it came to pass after these things, that Joshua the son of Nun, the servant of the LORD, died, being an hundred and ten years old. And they buried him in the border of his inheritance in Timnathserah, which is in mount Ephraim, on the north side of the hill of Gaash. And Israel served the LORD all the days of Joshua, and all the days of the elders that overlived Joshua, and which had known all the works of the LORD, that he had done for Israel.*
> *—Joshua 24:29–31*

Joshua's gravestone was a reminder of the faithfulness of God, how God honored and blessed this man who served Him. It reminds you and me that if we are faithful and obedient to God and we serve the Lord, He will do great things in our lives, just as He did for Joshua. The main character in the book of Joshua is not Joshua; it is God. This book is about the mighty acts God accomplished through Joshua. Just as God was with Moses, He was with Joshua (Joshua 1:5).

Frankly, I need this message. I can't help but think of the great man I am following as Senior Pastor of my church. He was a uniquely used servant of the Lord, a true soldier for Christ. Dr. Earl M. Johnson, Jr., was saved while serving in the military during the Korean War. He saw action while serving in a MASH unit and took part in the Chosin campaign. I remarked to Pastor Johnson one time that when he was converted to Christ, he simply switched armies. He served the Lord with all the courage and passion of a wartime soldier, and God used him to influence the lives of many.

When I think of following in his footsteps, it can be intimidating. However, when I remember the promise God gave Joshua—"as I was with Moses, so I will be with thee" (Joshua 1:5)—I am greatly encouraged. It wasn't Moses who accomplished great victories; it was God. God would do for Joshua what He did for Moses. Similarly, God will do for me what He did for Pastor Johnson, if I walk in obedience and faith like Pastor Johnson did. I can't be him, but I can be faithful, and so can you. Then God will do great things for you and me.

2. Secondly, there was a gravestone of fulfillment.

And the bones of Joseph, which the children of Israel brought up out of Egypt, buried they in Shechem, in a parcel of ground which Jacob bought of the sons of Hamor the father of Shechem for an hundred pieces of silver: and it became the inheritance of the children of Joseph.
—Joshua 24:32

They buried the bones of Joseph at Shechem as their ancestors had promised many years before. They had carried them through the desert wilderness and protected them in all the battles they had fought to conquer the land. Now the bones of Joseph were at rest in the land of his fathers, just as he had asked (Genesis 50:24–26).

And Eleazar the son of Aaron died; and they buried him in a hill that pertained to Phinehas his son, which was given him in mount Ephraim.

—Joshua 24:33

While he was alive, Joseph reminded God's people that God was going to deliver them from Egypt and bring them into the promised land. Joseph believed in God's promise to such a degree that he demanded they take his bones with them and bury him in that land. God fulfilled His Word and honored the desire of Joseph's heart. I imagine that if the people of Israel listened very carefully, they could hear Joseph's bones say, "I told you so!" God fulfills the desires of our hearts above and beyond our expectations.

3. Eleazar's grave was a gravestone of finality.

His death marked the changing of the guard in Israel. All of the old-timers, all those who came out of Egypt and out of the wilderness and saw God do mighty deeds, were then gone.

The end of an era is just the beginning of a new one. It's a sad moment when an old soldier of the Lord passes away. There's a huge empty spot to fill. It's especially sad when the people left behind don't pick up the mantle and move forward.

> *And also all that generation were gathered unto their fathers: and there arose another generation after them, which knew not the LORD, nor yet the works which he had done for Israel. And the children of Israel did evil in the sight of the LORD, and served Baalim....*
>
> *—Judges 2:10–11*

Nobody picked up the mantle. Nobody stepped up. Moses was dead. Joshua was dead. But their God was and still is alive. In the book of Judges, the Israelites would fall away from the Lord time after time, but He never deserted them. Every time they cried out to God, He would raise up wise judges to save them and lead them back to Him—Ehud, Deborah, Gideon, Jephthah, and Samson.

As Christians, we know the end of the story. Victory in Christ is assured. He will return to rule in justice and righteousness. But every generation needs godly leaders to set the standards and show the way. Who will step up? Who will share God's power and the glory? Who will pay the price of holiness and sacrifice and service? Are you willing to fill the gap? If you are, God will be with you as He was with Moses and as He was with Joshua.

WORKBOOK

Chapter Twelve Questions

Question: Why is complacency such a struggle, especially in prosperous times? What are some ways you can guard against an attitude of complacency and not take your salvation or your inheritance in Christ for granted?

_____

_____

_____

_____

_____

_____

_____

_____

_____

_____

Question: The Israelites turned from following the true God within only one generation. When you look at the generation coming after your own, do you see knowledge of the Bible and understanding of the gospel? If not, why? What are some practical ways you can help to pass on the faith, and why is it vital that every believer do so?

_____

_____

_____

_____

_____

_____

_____

_____

_____

_____

Journal: If you were going to share last words with your family, friends, church, or country, what would they be? How would you sum up the messages God has put on your heart? How can you be busy proclaiming those truths throughout your life?

_____

_____

_____

_____

_____

_____

_____

_____

_____

_____

Action: Find or make a sign with Joshua 24:15. What extra significance does this verse hold when you understand the life of Joshua and the context of his declaration? Place your sign in a prominent location in your home. If you have children, talk with them about what this verse meant to Israel and what it means to your family now.

Chapter Twelve Notes

_____

_____

_____

_____

_____

_____

_____

_____

_____

_____

_____

_____

_____

_____

_____

_____

_____

_____

_____

_____

_____

_____

_____

_____

REFERENCES

Notes

1. Stallone, Sylvester. *Rocky Balboa*. Sony Pictures Releasing, 2006.

2. Eisenhower, Dwight D. "Transcript of General Dwight D. Eisenhower's Order of the Day (1944)." Our Documents.Gov. https://www.ourdocuments.gov/doc.php?flash=false&doc=75&page =transcript.

3. Wood, Bryant G. "Carbon 14 Dating at Jericho." 2008. Bible Archaeology.org, 2008. https://biblearchaeology.org/research/ conquest-of-canaan/4051-carbon-14-dating-at-jericho?highlight=Wy JqZXJpY2hvIiwiamVyaWNob3J   dzIiwiamVyaWNobyciLCInamVya WNobyIsIidqZXJpY2hvJyJd.

4. Wiersbe, Warren W. *Be Strong*. Victor Books, 1996, p. 10.

5. Wiersbe, *Be Strong*, p. 11–12.

6. Farrar, Steve. *Battle Ready: Prepare to Be Used by God*. David C. Cook, 2009, p. 89.

7. Scott, Robert, Liddell, Henry George. *A Greek-English Lexicon*.

Macmillan and Company, 1869, p. 824.

8. Klein, Ernest. *A Comprehensive Etymological Dictionary of the Hebrew Language*. Macmillan Publishing Company, 1987.

9. Churchill, Winston. Quoted in Frasier McAlpine, "50 Sir Winston Churchill Quotes to Live By." BBC America. 2015. http://www.bbcamerica.com/anglophenia/2015/04/50-churchill-quotes.

10. *Encyclopaedia Britanica*, "Walking Purchase." https://www.britannica.com/event/Walking-Purchase.

11. Redpath, Alan. *Victorious Living*. Revell, 1993.

12. Wiersbe, *Be Strong*, p. 23.

13. History.com "This Day in History: April 12, 1945: FDR Dies." 2019. https://www.history.com/this-day-in-history/fdr-dies.

14. Llyod-Jones, D. Martyn. *I Am Not Ashamed: Advice to Timothy*. Baker Book House, 1986, p. 162.

15. Packer, J. I. *Knowing God*. InterVarsity Press, 2011, p. 23.

16. Packer, *Knowing God*.

17. McMillen, S. I. *None of These Diseases*. Commission Press, 1979.

18. Depree, Max. *Leadership Is an Art*. Crown Publishing Group, 2011, p. 14.

19. *Merriam-Webster Dictionary*, "encourage." https://www.merriam-webster.com/dictionary/encourage.

20. Paul R. House. *1, 2 Kings*. Vol. 8. Broadman & Holman Publishers, 1995, p. 110.

21. Donald Slager, *A Handbook on 1 & 2 Kings*. Vol. 1–2. United Bible Societies, 2008, p. 111.

22. Pink, Arthur W. *Gleanings from Joshua*. Moody Press, 1964, p. 46–47.

23. Pink, *Gleanings from Joshua*, p. 47.

24. Engstrom, Ted. *The Making of a Christian Leader*. Zondervan, 1978, p. 95.

25. *Today in the Word* (May 1996), p. 24.

26. Schulz, Charles. *Classic Peanuts*. January 9, 2011. https://www.gocomics.com/peanuts/2011/01/09#.UxK1_-NmNQT.

27. Wood, Bryant. "The Walls of Jericho: Archaeology Confirms: They Really Did Come A-tumblin' Down." Answers in Genesis. March 1, 1999. https://answersingenesis.org/archaeology/the-walls-of-jericho/.

28. Boice, James Montgomery. *Joshua*. Baker Books, 2006, p. 32.

29. Boice, *Joshua*, p. 31.

30. ten Boom, Corrie. *The Hiding Place*. 1971. Hendrickson Publishers, 2009.

31. Wiersbe, *Be Strong*, p. 36.

32. *Encyclopedia of Religion*, "Cannanite Religion: An Overview." https://www.encyclopedia.com/environment/encyclopedias-almanacs-transcripts-and-maps/canaanite-religion-overview.

33. Elwell, Walter A., and Philip Wesley Comfort. *Tyndale Bible Dictionary*. Tyndale House Publishers, 2001, p. 255.

34. Steiner, Beth. "Canaanite Religion," *The Lexham Bible Dictionary*. Lexham Press, 2016.

35. *Lexico*, "volition." https://www.lexico.com/definition/volition.

36. H. Lynn Gardner. *Commending and Defending Christian Faith:*

An Introduction to Christian Apologetics. College Press Publishing Co., 2010, p. 203.

37. Wiersbe, *Be Strong*, p. 49.

38. "The Charles Blondin Story." Creative Bible Study. https://www.creativebiblestudy.com/Blondin-story.html.

39. Long, V. Phillips. "Joshua 3:15 Study Note." *ESV Study Bible*. Crossway, 2008, p. 398.

40. C. H. Spurgeon. *The Metropolitan Tabernacle Pulpit Sermons*. Vol. 37. Passmore & Alabaster, 1891, p. 331.

41. *Eerdmans Dictionary of the Bible*, "Adam." Edited by David Noel Freedman, Allen C. Myers, and Astrid B. Beck. W. B. Eerdmans, 2000, p. 19.

42. Campbell, Donald K. *The Bible Knowledge Commentary: An Exposition of the Scriptures*. Vol. 1. Victor Books, 1985, p. 335.

43. Campbell, *Bible Knowledge Commentary*, p. 335.

44. "Facing the Impossible." Preaching Today. https://www.preachingtoday.com/illustrations/2001/september/13260.html.

45. Boice, *Joshua*, p. 39.

46. Strong, James. "Strong's Hebrew #1537: Gilgal." *A Concise Dictionary of the Words in the Greek Testament and the Hebrew Bible*. Faithlife, 2019.

47. Schaeffer, Francis. *Joshua and the Flow of Biblical History*. Crossway, 2004.

48. Wood, "The Walls of Jericho."

49. *Merriam-Webster Dictionary*, "stronghold." https://www.merri

am-webster.com/dictionary/stronghold.

50. Williamson, Porter B. *General Patton's Principles for Life and Leadership*. Management & Systems Consultants (MSC), 2009.

51. Wiersbe, *Be Strong*, p. 90.

52. Boice, *Joshua*, p. 53–54.

53. Swanson, James. *Dictionary of Biblical Languages with Semantic Domains: Hebrew (Old Testament)*. Logos Research Systems, 1997.

54. Calvin, John, and Henry Beveridge. *Commentary on the Book of Joshua*. Logos Bible Software, 2010, p. 96.

55. "Hiroo Onoda, the Soldier Who Refused to Surrender, 1974." Rare Historical Photos. 2017. https://rarehistoricalphotos.com/hiroo-onoda-1974/.

56. Strong, James. "Strong's Hebrew #5911: akowr." *A Concise Dictionary of the Words in the Greek Testament and the Hebrew Bible*. Faithlife, 2019.

57. Strong, James. "Strong's Hebrew #5912: akan." *A Concise Dictionary of the Words in the Greek Testament and the Hebrew Bible*. Faithlife, 2019.

58. Smith, James E. *History of Israel*. Lulu.com, 2012, p. 30.

59. Posnanski, Joe. "An Injury Suffered in Celebration Is No Less Painful Than Any Other." *Sports Illustrated*. May 30, 2010. https://www.si.com/more-sports/2010/05/30/kendry-morales.

60. Wiersbe, *Be Strong*, p. 87.

61. Louw, Johannes P., and Eugene Albert Nida. *Greek-English Lexicon of the New Testament: Based on Semantic Domains*. United Bible Societies, 1996, p. 744–745.

62. Bruce, F. F., R. K. Harrison, and Ronald F. Youngblood, eds. *Nelson's Illustrated Bible Dictionary*. New and enhanced edition. Thomas Nelson, 2014.

63. Wight, Fred. *Manners and Customs of Bible Lands*. Billy Graham Evangelistic Association, 1994.

64. Boice, *Joshua*, p. 66.

65. Meyer, Frederick Brotherton. *Joshua, and the Land of Promise*. Fleming H. Revell, 1893, p. 115.

66. Bible Lessons International. "The Conquest of the Promised Land: Joshua 9." Bible.org. 2012. https://bible.org/seriespage/joshua-9.

67. Campbell, Donald K. *Joshua: Leader Under Fire*. Victor Books, 1981, p. 78.

68. Boice, *Joshua*, p. 80.

69. Swanson, James. *Dictionary of Biblical Languages with Semantic Domains: Hebrew (Old Testament)*. Logos Research Systems, 1997.

70. International Council on Biblical Inerrancy. "The Chicago Statement on Biblical Inerrancy." 1978. https://www.etsjets.org/files/documents/Chicago_Statement.pdf.

71. Grudem, Wayne A. *Systematic Theology: An Introduction to Biblical Doctrine*. Inter-Varsity Press; Zondervan Pub. House, 2004, p. 315.

72. Grudem, *Systematic Theology*, p. 355.

73. Gill, John. "Joshua 10:13." *Gill's Exposition of the Whole Bible*. In BibleHub: Commentaries. https://biblehub.com/commentaries/joshua/10-13.htm.

74. Olcott, W. T. *Sun Lore of All Ages: A Collection of Myths and Legends Concerning the Sun and Its Worship.* G. P. Putnam's Sons, 1914.

75. Boyd, Robert T. *Boyd's Bible Handbook.* Cross reference edition. Harvest House Publisher, 1982, p. 122–123.

76. Spence-Jones, H. D. M., ed. *Joshua.* The Pulpit Commentary. Funk & Wagnalls Company, 1909.

77. Jamieson, R., A. R. Fausset, and D. Brown. *Commentary Critical and Explanatory on the Whole Bible.* Vol. 1. Logos Research Systems, 1997, p. 151.

78. Josephus, F., Whiston, W. *The Works of Josephus: Complete and Unabridged.* Hendrickson, 1987, p. 130.

79. Walton, John. "Biblical Credibility and Joshua 10: What Does the Bible Really Claim?" 2013. https://biologos.org/articles/biblical-credibility-and-joshua-10-what-does-the-text-really-claim.

80. Wilson, Robert Dick. "What Does The Sun Stood Still Mean?" *Moody Monthly.* October 1920.

81. Blair, Hugh J. "Joshua," *The New Bible Commentary Revised.* Third edition. Inter-Varsity Press, 1970, p. 244.

82. Archer, Gleason. *Encyclopedia of Bible Difficulties.* Zondervan, 1982, p. 161.

83. Campbell, *Bible Knowledge Commentary*, p. 351.

84. "Solar Storm Slows Earth's Daily Cycle by Several Milliseconds." *Wisconsin State Journal* 217, no. 260 (May 8, 1973). https://newspaperarchive.com/madison-wisconsin-state-journal-may-08-1973-p-1/.

85. Gateway Worship. "Revelation Song," track 7 on *Living for You.*

Integrity Music, 2006.

86. Louw and Nida, *Greek-English Lexicon*, p. 801–802.

87. "What Wondrous Love Is This." https://hymnary.org/text/what_wondrous_love_is_this_o_my_soul_o_m.

88. Marisfield, H. P. "Joshua: Victory Through Faith." *The Christian Expositor: A Verse-by-Verse Exposition of the Scriptures.* Logos Publications, p. 114. http://www.christadelphian.or.tz/sites/default/files/joshua_-_expositor.pdf.

89. Marisfield, "Joshua: Victory Through Faith."

90. Green, Jay P., and Maurice A. Robinson. "H6504: parad." *A Concise Lexicon to the Biblical Languages.* Sovereign Grace Publishers, 2000, p. 194.

91. Holladay, William Lee, and Ludwig Köhler. *A Concise Hebrew and Aramaic Lexicon of the Old Testament.* Brill, 2000, p. 139.

92. Cruden, Alexander, and Roswell D. Hitchcock. *Hitchcock's New and Complete Analysis of the Holy Bible: Including Cruden's Concordance to the Holy Scriptures.* Cosimo, 2011.

93. Abarim Publications. "Debir." https://www.abarim-publications.com/Meaning/Debir.html.

94. Your Dictionary. "What Are Some Facts About Edmund Hillary?" https://biography.yourdictionary.com/articles/what-are-some-facts-about-edmund-hillary.html.

95. Towns, Elmer. *Fasting with the Lord's Prayer: Experience a Deeper and More Powerful Relationship with God.* Baker Books, 2014.

96. Strong, James. "Strong's Hebrew #2275: Chebrown." *A Concise Dictionary of the Words in the Greek Testament and the Hebrew*

Bible. Faithlife, 2019.

97. "Wholly follow the Lord" comes from two Hebrew words: *male* (to fill) and *ahar* (after or behind, in place). Thus, the idea of filling in the place behind—closing the gap.

See: Kaiser, Walter C. "1195 מָלֵא." *Theological Wordbook of the Old Testament*. Edited by R. Laird Harris, Gleason L. Archer Jr., and Bruce K. Waltke. Moody Press, 1999, p. 505.

See also: Harris, R. Laird. "68 אַחַר,"." *Theological Wordbook of the Old Testament*. Edited by R. Laird Harris, Gleason L. Archer Jr., and Bruce K. Waltke. Moody Press, 1999, p. 33.

98. Howat, Irene. *Jim Elliot: He Is No Fool*. Christian Focus Publications, 2005.

99. Steer, Roger. *Basic Christian: The Inside Story of John Stott*. InterVarsity Press, 2010.

100. Ravi Zacharias. *Jesus Among Other Gods*. Thomas Nelson, 2002, p. 58.

101. Grooms, Mike. "Connecting Through the Word: Am I Claiming and Enjoying My Inheritance? 'Give Me This Mountain' Joshua 11-22." Rainbow Forest Baptist Church: Sermon Notes. June 10, 2018.

102. Pink, *Gleanings from Joshua*, p. 360.

103. Grooms, "Connecting Through the Word."

104. Morgan, Robert J. *Nelson's Complete Book of Stories, Illustrations, and Quotes*. Electronic edition. Thomas Nelson Publishers, 2000, p. 515–516.

105. Spurgeon, Charles. *John Ploughman's Talks*. Baker, 1976.

106. Walker, W. L. "Presume, Presumptuous, Presumptuously." *The International Standard Bible Encyclopaedia*. The Howard-Severance Company, 1915, p. 2438.

107. Louw and Nida, *Greek-English Lexicon*, p. 660.

108. *Etymonline*, "mortify." https://www.etymonline.com/word/mortify.

109. Kapic, Kelly M., and Wesley Vander Lugt. *Pocket Dictionary of the Reformed Tradition*. IVP Academic, 2013, p. 76.

110. Warfield, B. B. *Perfectionism*. Vol. 2. 1931. Baker, 1981, p. 561.

111. Owen, John. *The Mortification of Sin: A Puritan's View of How to Deal with Sin in Your Life*. Christian Focus Publication, 2010, p. 59.

112. Owen, Mortification, p. 63.

113. Louw and Nida, *Greek-English Lexicon*, p. 660.

114. Owen, Mortification, p. 66–67.

115. Heiser, Michael S., and Vincent M. Setterholm. *Glossary of Morpho-Syntactic Database Terminology*. Lexham Press, 2013, p. 2013.

116. John Owen, *Sin and Temptation: The Challenge of Personal Godliness*. Bethany House Publishers, 1996, p. 159.

117. Heiser and Setterholm, *Glossary of Morpho-Syntactic Database Terminology*, p. 2013.

118. Nack, Bill. "Pure Heart." *Sports Illustrated*, June 4, 1990. https://vault.si.com/vault/1990/06/04/pure-heart-in-waging-the-most-glorious-triple-crown-campaign-ever-secretariat-made-racing-history-in-the-doing-he-took-the-author-on-an-unforgettably-exhilarating-ride.

119. Owen, Mortification, p. 173.

120. Owen, John. *Triumph Over Temptation*. Victor Books, 2005, p. 85.

121. Hession, Roy. *Broken People, Transforming Grace: The Gospel's Message of Saving Love.* CLC Publications, 2016.

122. Owen, Mortification, p. 174–176.

123. Stevenson, George J. *The Methodist Hymn-Book and Its Associations.* Hamilton, Adams, & Co., 1870, p. 97. https://www.lifeway.com/en/articles/the-story-behind-jesus-love-of-my-soul-hymnal-history.

124. Hunton, William Lee. *Stories of Favorite Hymns: The Origin, Authorship, and Use of Hymns We Love.* General Council Publication House, 1917.

125. Luther, Martin. *D. Martin Luthers Werke (Weimarer Ausgabe)* 11.223.

126. Luther, Martin. *D. Martin Luthers Werke (Weimarer Ausgabe)* 10.11.181.

127. Luther, Martin. *D. Martin Luthers Werke (Weimarer Ausgabe)* 10.11.80.

128. Boice, *Joshua*, p. 128–129.

129. Campbell, *Joshua, Leadership Under Fire*, p. 117.

130. Boice, *Joshua*, p. 150.

131. Berman, Sara J. "What Is Manslaughter? What Is Murder Vs. Manslaughter?" Nolo. https://www.nolo.com/legal-encyclopedia/homicide-murder-manslaughter-32637-2.html.

132. Ironside, H. A. *Joshua.* Loizeaux Brothers, 1961, p. 129–130.

133. Morris, Henry M. "Cities of Refuge." September 29, 2007. *Days of Praise.* https://www.icr.org/article/cities-refuge/.

134. Bridge to the Bible, "6 Cities of Refuge." 2015.

https://www.bridgetothebible.com/Bible%20Lists/6%20cities%20of%20refuge.htm.

135. Morris, Henry M. "Cities of Refuge." Days of Praise, 2007. https://www.icr.org/article/cities-refuge/.

136. Bridge to the Bible, "6 Cities of Refuge."

137. Morris, "Cities of Refuge."

138. Hastings, James. *A Dictionary of the Bible*. Vol. 2. Charles Scribner's Sons, 1902.

139. Inman, Thomas. *History: Ancient Faiths Embodied in Ancient Names*. Reprinted Nabu Press, 1872, p. 551.

140. Boice, *Joshua*, p. 154.

141. Mendelson, Levi. "Cities of Refuge Demystified." Chabad. https://www.chabad.org/parshah/article_cdo/aid/2684913/jewish/Cities-of-Refuge-Demystified.htm.

142. Boice, *Joshua*, p. 154.

143. Wesley, Charles. "Thou, Oh Christ, Art All I Want." https://hymnary.org/text/thou_o_christ_art_all_i_want.

144. MacArthur, Douglas. "Farewell Address to Congress." April 19, 1951. American Rhetoric. https://www.americanrhetoric.com/speeches/douglasmacarthurfarewelladdress.htm.

145. Strong, James. "Strong's Hebrew #5647: abad." *A Concise Dictionary of the Words in the Greek Testament and the Hebrew Bible*. Faithlife, 2019.

146. Campbell, *Bible Knowledge Commentary*, p. 137–138.

About the Author

Dr. Jerry R. Harmon, a native of Baltimore, Maryland, is the Senior Pastor of Grace Bible Baptist Church and President of Faith Theological Seminary of Catonsville, MD. He was educated at Mid-America Baptist Theological Seminary in Memphis, TN, where he received a Master of Divinity and a Ph.D. majoring in Hebrew and OT with minors in NT Greek and Theology. Dr. Harmon also did graduate studies in Hebrew at Johns Hopkins University in his hometown. Dr. Harmon has lectured and preached in seminaries and churches in the U.S. and all over the world. Dr. Harmon enjoys participating in annual archaeology digs in Israel, lecturing or serving as an adjunct in various seminaries, spending time with his family, working with the church staff, and getting to know the people who make up the large congregation of Grace Bible Baptist Church.

About Sermon To Book

SermonToBook.com began with a simple belief: that sermons should be touching lives, *not* collecting dust. That's why we turn sermons into high-quality books that are accessible to people all over the globe.

Turning your sermon series into a book exposes more people to God's Word, better equips you for counseling, accelerates future sermon prep, adds credibility to your ministry, and even helps make ends meet during tight times.

John 21:25 tells us that the world itself couldn't contain the books that would be written about the work of Jesus Christ. Our mission is to try anyway. Because in heaven, there will no longer be a need for sermons or books. Our time is now.

If God so leads you, we'd love to work with you on your sermon or sermon series.

Visit www.sermontobook.com to learn more.

Made in the USA
Middletown, DE
07 June 2021

40758036R00166